Louis I. Kahn

Unbuilt Masterworks

Louis I. Kahn

Unbuilt Masterworks

Kent Larson

Foreword by Vincent Scully

Afterword by William J. Mitchell

THE MONACELLI PRESS

For Beth and Olivia

First published in the United States of America in 2000 by
The Monacelli Press, Inc.
10 East 92nd Street, New York, New York 10128.

Library of Congress Cataloging-in-Publication Data
Larson, Kent.
Louis I. Kahn : unbuilt masterworks / Kent Larson ;
foreword by Vincent Scully ; afterword by William J. Mitchell.
p.   cm.
Includes bibliographical references.
ISBN 1-58093-014-X
1. Kahn, Louis I., 1901–1974—Criticism and interpretation.
2. Architectural drawing—20th century—United States.
I. Kahn, Louis I., 1901–1974. II. Title.
NA737.K32L37   1999
720'.22'22—dc21
98-52140

Printed and bound in China

Designed by Fahrenheit

Contents

Foreword

Vincent Scully

It seems a long time since Louis Kahn died. A lot has happened in architecture since then, some of it very good, some of it appalling—and each of us has a different idea about which is which. But all of it makes Kahn's work look better than ever on its own terms, better in its solidity, its gravity. Above all, I suppose, in its timeless air. Kahn always said he was interested in "beginnings," and it is something like that we feel in his architecture, some solemn archaic presence, some paternal power, as if he was familiar with the work of the father of us all.

"Here is a man for you to look at," wrote Louis Sullivan of H. H. Richardson's Marshall Field Warehouse, "in a world of barren pettiness, a male." The nineteenth century's admiration for what is called "masculinity" in architecture is not popular today, nor is the sexist metaphor agreeable in general. But no deprecation of women need be involved in a perception of the paternal qualities of Kahn's architecture: ponderous, firm, hard, protective it is, and in terms of intrinsic structure, the very image of law, of justice unswerving. The old Roman words of the cult of the father are still the best ones to describe it: *auctoritas*, *gravitas*, even *Romanitas*. I remember the great Frank Brown standing on the ruins of the Roman rostrum at the colony of Cosa more than forty years ago, saying that the most appropriate word to describe Roman architecture was "authority." That has not been a popular word either, then or now. But it was Frank Brown who introduced Louis Kahn to Roman ruins as living architecture a long half-century ago, and it was the ruins that helped shape almost all of Kahn's greatest buildings thereafter, foremost among them the great unbuilt projects of Luanda, Mikveh Israel, and Hurva that Kent Larson has so magically caused to rise up before our eyes.

The U.S. Consulate in Luanda, Angola, is effectively the first of them, and in its burgeoning *Romanitas* we also have to feel the liberating effect upon Kahn of the young architect Robert Venturi; his relationship with the older man came to be almost as torn between respect and resentment on both sides as that between a strong father and a strong son. A comparison of dates shows us that Venturi, who first went to Rome in 1948, preceded Kahn in projecting the use of Roman ruins as deep screens around his buildings, as in the Pearson house project of 1957. Venturi could do so without feelings of guilt precisely because he had gone to architecture school at Princeton where, in his day, Bauhaus iconoclasm had not yet penetrated: no onus was involved in a direct employment of historical forms. Venturi had been trained by the same kind of French modern-classical architect who had taught Kahn at Penn some twenty years earlier, but Kahn had been forced in the meantime to bear the impact of high modernist dogma, and he needed to be freed from it in order to find his own underlying conceptual structure once more.

So the reuse of Rome started with Luanda but did not, as yet, go very deep. The concrete planes, penetrated by Hadrianic keyholes, are flat screens, as Venturi's had been. They were not yet rounded out into great cylinders, the swelling curved planes that formed some of the grandest of Roman spaces. That first happened in the meeting house of the Salk Institute. It was indeed of that project that Kahn first spoke of "wrapping ruins around buildings." And so he did, setting up noble sequences of flat and curved walls penetrated by unglazed voids, such as modern architecture had not yet seen. With them Kahn reconquered a volumetric dimension long abandoned by modernism; he revived Rome. But it was always the Rome of the ruin, because he consistently refused to employ classical details, as some of his strongest descendants—among whom I include not only Venturi but also the Ricardo Bofill of about 1980 and the late, bitterly lamented Aldo Rossi—were prepared to do. This was true in part because Kahn always remained a high modernist and wished to seem to reinvent everything afresh in every building.[1] So the ruins were an excellent disguise for a fundamentally classical sensibility.

But they were more than that. Their harsh rigor, their primitive starkness, created exactly the sense of "beginnings" that Kahn was after. In this he was a true romanticist-classicist, another Piranesi, and was indeed going back to the very beginnings of modern architecture, to what the eighteenth century called the "sublime," since it was the sense of awe, terror, and rude grandeur that he wanted to reproduce. But the unadorned leanness of his concrete planes also created the taut aliveness, the stretched tension, that is central to the vitality of his work. His walls are not thick like those of Rome but thin like those of Le Corbusier; yet he deploys them in layered shells that are suggestive of great Roman depth.

Larson's re-creations show all this supremely well. They lead us into Kahn's own majestic ruins, true ghosts called up out of the air. Mikveh Israel Synagogue is especially poignant in that regard. Here Kahn's cylindrical towers shape a true miracle of light as it penetrates the towers from outside and is filtered through them into the large central meeting space of the interior. In the 1960s a scholar at the American Academy in Rome showed, to his satisfaction at least, that the Forum Baths at Ostia had been built without glass, so effective was the southern orientation and the hypocaust heating under the floor. There can be little doubt that this sanctioned for Kahn his first use, at the Salk, of curved walls with unglazed arched openings in them. There, though, the second layer of walls, screened by them, was glazed. But the big holes in Mikveh Israel's exterior walls would have required glazing, and Kahn's attempts to solve that problem, reconstructed by Larson from some of Kahn's drawings, show us how deadly serious the use of glazing was in terms of the integrity, the credibility, of the building as a whole. In the end, Kahn's flat mullioned planes of glass, set well within the curving planes of the cylindrical walls, look as if they simply should not be there. Could not Kahn have gone ahead and fitted curved planes of glass into the openings? Another architect might have done so, but it was impossible for Kahn. He would have felt that he had to distinguish between the two irreconcilable conditions, the pure void and the protective membrane, and he does so with some style. But it does not entirely convince us of its rightness, and it seems likely that Kahn himself did not like it very much either.

The problem was even more difficult in the Hurva Synagogue; as Larson tells us, the word itself means "ruins." The first scheme, which remains, I believe, the supremely great one, utterly defies glazing. It is itself a great city in ruin standing in light. If only it could have been built that way, rising transcendent upon all the layers of old synagogues buried below it. It could have evoked the ultimate image out of Ezekiel, the new city rising after the destruction of all other cities, celebrating the site of ruin, Judaism unconquerable after all the conquests and burnings. It would have risen above Jerusalem, an ultimate shrine of indestructible pylons and walls, a wonder of silence and light, open imperishably to the winds and the rain and the assaults of time, to Jehovah's blazing sun and his lightning flash. Of course all that could never be. And one wonders if Kahn would ever have been able to tame that first vision and enclose it in a satisfying way. The grand jagged light of that first project is hardly matched by the blander illumination of the rectangular masses of the third, where Kahn brought it all closer to glazable form. He even created a concrete cloud of girder billowing over the sanctuary—like the low cloud-ceiling of the Palazzo dei Congressi in Venice—and a vast horizontal sweep at a floor level under the enormous beams.

Whatever we think, Larson limns the space and light of both projects so tellingly that we can almost inhabit them ourselves and perhaps even decide which we prefer—if indeed it is necessary to do so. Kahn may well have had resources of invention we don't dream of and might have worked it all out in some way we can hardly imagine now. He always worked long and hard on every project, driving some clients crazy with impatience as he turned every form over and over in his brain, bathed in the light of his imagination. But it is hard to believe that anything could ever have been more splendid and full of awe, more wholly sublime in every sense, than the first project for Hurva, drawing together as it does the pylons of the temples of Pharaonic Egypt and the square sanctuaries of the Ancient East. Here, as Larson brings him alive for us at the climactic moment of his Jewishness, Kahn makes us deal with something more than the vast self-satisfactions of Rome. The sharply sloping walls shaping deep space, the blinding light of day slashing between the pylons, all finally embody a religious passion far fiercer than Rome's, and a father more terrible even than Rome could imagine.

Unbuilt Ruins

I thought of the beauty of ruins . . . of things which nothing lives behind . . . and so I thought of wrapping ruins around buildings.

—Louis I. Kahn

Louis I. Kahn was an architect of beautiful contradictions. He had profound faith and respect for the individual but created architectural elements out of scale with the human figure. He practiced the highest form of modern architecture even as he looked to the ancient world for inspiration. His buildings are experienced as rich and elegant but are constructed of basic, often crude materials. His work consists almost exclusively of secular buildings yet includes the most sacred of spaces. This study attempts to shed light on the mystery of how Kahn came to make the architecture that he did by looking in depth at the projects he could not build.

The story is well known. Kahn, having built little of note by the age of fifty, spends four months as architect in residence at the American Academy in Rome. During this time he experiences the great ruins of the ancient world and resolves that "the architecture of Italy will remain as the inspirational source of the works of the future."[1] He returns to the United States in 1951 to execute his first major commission and struggles for the next twenty-three years to incorporate into his work the lessons learned in Italy, Greece, and Egypt. In the process he redefines modern architecture and becomes one of the most important architects of the second half of the twentieth century. He dies at the height of his career after building many of the master-works of our time: the Kimbell Art Museum, the laboratories of the Salk Institute, the Phillips Exeter Academy library, the Yale Center for British Art, and his monumental projects on the Indian subcontinent.

The actual story is much more complicated, of course. Kahn had many other influences, and his early years prepared him well for mid-life revelations. Kahn also, to our regret, left far too many important works unbuilt. Between 1959 and 1963, he used a series of fascinating unbuilt projects—particularly the U.S. Consulate in Luanda, Angola, the meeting house of the Salk Institute, and the Mikveh Israel Synagogue—to develop and test his new ideas. At the end of the 1960s he created what is perhaps the clearest expression of his architectural link to the

1. Colosseum.
Rome, Italy. 72–80 C.E.

old world—the Hurva Synagogue for Jerusalem. In all of these projects, Kahn explored elements later found in his built work: a configuration of space as discrete volumes, complex ambient light and shadow, a celebration of mass and structure, the use of materials with both modernist and archaic qualities, monumental openings uncompromised by frames, and his concept of "ruins wrapped around buildings." Finally, the unbuilt Palazzo dei Congressi in Venice prefigured a significant change in direction, as evidenced by his last major built work, the Yale Center for British Art in New Haven, Connecticut.

The computer-graphics images contained in this book attempt to capture something of Kahn's genius: the ability to incorporate the spirit of the archaic and the deep understanding of fundamentals into a timeless, styleless architectural vision. But how does one approach the problem? As William J. Mitchell asks in his afterword, "What are the rules of this curious game?" We now have the ability to create virtually any image conceivable, but there are few good precedents for the application of new visualization tools to the study of architectural history.

Do we proceed in the conservative manner of the archaeologist, taking care to differentiate between verifiable evidence and speculation—as old and new material is distinguished in the reconstruction of a Greek vase? Alternately, should we consider the incomplete evidence left by Kahn to be the score of a performance, where personal interpretation is permitted? At what point does the resolution of form and the addition of detail cause the design to become less the work of Kahn than invention? Is it prudent to establish the synthetic nature of the image through conceptual, non-perspectival sections and isometrics, or impossible views like the section-perspective? Do we create ambiguous imagery, as Kahn did in his design process, with grainy black-and-white photographs of physical models that highlight essential elements and obscure missing detail? Do we aim for the suspension of disbelief and the illusion of reality? Can we indulge in what the modernists deride as "conceits of perspective"—individual and fleeting glimpses of architecture from a single point in space and time? Should we use this radiosity-based computer-graphics rendering technology as synthetic photography, or does the unlimited control and range of effects make it more like painting, or perhaps some new hybrid? I grappled with these questions throughout this investigation. Ultimately, I established the primary goal: to create new imagery that communicates Kahn's unbuilt space as it might have been experienced while relying on the archival material to explain the plan, elevation, detail, and overall form. These new studies focus on what the archival material does not reveal—the complex play of form, light, and materials fundamental to all of Kahn's later built work.

Although the representations in this book are based on the best available archival evidence, we will never know how Kahn would have actually built any of his unbuilt work. All would have evolved further had the design process not been aborted—but the ideas, brilliant and clear, deserve to be better understood. To the extent that these speculations fall short of Kahn's ideal, they should be considered my personal impressions of what might have been.

Ancient Light/Luminous Interiors

The digital images in this book are, in large part, a study of Kahn's use of light. No other architect of the mid-twentieth century, with the exception of Le Corbusier at Ronchamp and La Tourette, was as successful in its manipulation as Kahn. The qualities of light Kahn experienced in the works of ancient Rome found their way into most of Kahn's built and unbuilt work: the dramatic patterns of light and shadow in the Colosseum (fig.1); the complex inter-reflected ambient light and shade of the Pantheon (fig. 2). That he referred again and again to the light of the Pantheon is not surprising—most find what Kahn found: "a world within a world,"[2] "the embodiment of the immeasurable . . . this light which almost cuts you like a knife."[3]

2. Interior of the Pantheon.
Rome, Italy, 120–124 C.E.

Entering the Pantheon from the chaotic streets of modern Rome is a startling experience for anyone sensitive to the play of light in space. The visitor is simultaneously struck by the circle of sky at the oculus, and by the white-hot disk of sunlight striking the dome. But this is only the obvious. As the observer becomes accustomed to the dim ambience, it becomes clear that, in effect, the sun does not light the interior. The "point source" of the sun would cast the sharpest of shadows, but in the Pantheon are the softest of ambient light and subtle gradations of grays to nearly black. The disk of reflected light creates the light to which we respond.

The path of light is extraordinarily complex in this ancient building. After striking interior surfaces within the area of the disk, sunlight scatters in directions determined by its position in space, the angle of incidence of the rays, and the texture of the surface it strikes. This diffused light continues to bounce from surface to surface until the energy becomes negligible. Shadows become softer and more luminous as diffuse interreflections fill in darkness. Surfaces that receive no direct light—and this is most of the space—are brightest when they are adjacent to those that do. The deepest of shadows are lit only by the soft dim glow of exhausted light from the final iterations of bouncing light. Each coffer of the dome has a unique orientation in space and relationship to the disk of sunlight—the pattern of shadows and the intensity of ambient light is different for each element, which results in the marvelous variation in shade and shadow. This intricate dance of light changes dramatically from hour to hour, season to season. It varies according to the haze and shimmers as clouds move overhead.

Our reaction to light in space is directly related to the physiognomy of our eyes and how information is processed in the brain. The main rotunda space at the Massachusetts Institute of Technology is very similar to the Pantheon in that it is enclosed by a coffered dome. But the quality of light is profoundly different. At MIT, the oculus is closed and does not bring light into the space, and the west facade contains vertical floor-to-soffit windows that bring horizontal light and glare into the space. Thus attention is drawn to the exterior and away from the interior space. In addition, eyes adjust to the intensity of light through the windows, closing the iris and obscuring the form, detail, and subtle light of the interior. The MIT space is flat and dull; the light of the Pantheon is luminous and ethereal.

Kahn understood the detrimental effects of glare and the mechanics of creating luminous interiors. His words were often as opaque as his architecture was clear and direct, but when he wrote about light, the images were vivid. With many variations, he found words to express his sensitivity to light and shadow in architecture:

> *And I thought all material being spent light.*
> *Light as a prevalence of the luminous, which I*
> *cannot conceive as being material, but entering a*
> *wild dance of flames itself and become material.*[4]

Kahn often described that mysterious process by which light, nothing more than imperceptible electromagnetic energy, comes alive when it strikes material and, in turn, enters our eyes. Likewise, the material forming such a work of architecture is only atoms until struck by photons. Kahn, at times, spoke of material and structure as, in effect, the source of light:

> *The room is the beginning of architecture. It is the*
> *place of the mind. You in the room with its*
> *dimensions, its structure, its light responds to its*
> *character, its spiritual aura . . . Structure, I*
> *believe is the giver of light.*[5]

At other times, depending on the subject, he would emphasize light as the source:

> *The Treasury of the Shadows, lying in ambiance,*
> *Light to Silence, Silence to Light. Light, the giver*
> *of presence, casts its shadow which belongs to*
> *Light. What is made belongs to Light and*
> *Desire.*[6]

The Yale University Art Gallery, Kahn's first commission after returning from Rome in 1951, reveals his first use of the luminous light found in the Pantheon. In the stairwell of the gallery, a clerestory ring of glass block brings diffused light onto the vertical surfaces of a concrete triangle; the light then filters down the curved concrete cylinder and up onto the flat concrete ceiling. As light weaves and reflects its way down through openings in the stair forms, softening shadows and reducing contrast, the viewer senses light becoming exhausted. There are no eye-level openings in the cylinder to introduce glare and distractions. In this small space, as in all of Kahn's work, the harsh and flattening effect of large areas of direct sunlight entering spaces roofed with glass is avoided.

Following the completion of the Yale Art Gallery, Kahn designed two projects that, although very important to his career, did not break new ground in the use of light. The Trenton bathhouse, with its square oculus set into pyramidal ceiling forms, seems to be a direct reference to the dome and oculus of the Pantheon, without capturing any of its kind of light. In contrast to the bright light introduced from the large horizontal exterior openings, the contribution of the oculus to the illumination is insignificant. Glare is not controlled. The Alfred Newton Richards Medical Research Building, at the University of Pennsylvania, did not work with natural lighting in any sophisticated way, nor did the less significant Tribune Review Publishing Company Building. Soon after, Kahn designed two unbuilt projects that were generated specifically to control light. The U.S. Consulate in Luanda, Angola, and the meeting house of the Salk Institute directly addressed the issue of glare but did not yet attempt to craft a luminous interior space.

Kahn's first sophisticated use of light in a major space can be found in the First Unitarian Church, where he both created a luminous interior and eliminated glare. To accomplish this, he placed a cubic light monitor in each of the four corners of the sanctuary—with the two glazed sides of the cube facing the inside corner of the sanctuary enclosure. In this way, direct light falls on the adjacent concrete surfaces and is diffused into the interior, while a direct view of the sky is prevented to eliminate glare. Subtle ambient light reflected off the concrete washes the inversely sloped ceiling and creates very soft shadows at the supporting columns. Although the interior form is simple, and the opportunity for light to surprise is more limited than in his later designs, the solution is extremely successful. With the design of the First Unitarian Church, Kahn seems finally to have arrived at an architectural solution that actually creates the luminous light of the Pantheon.

The question arises: why did Kahn take almost ten years after returning from Rome to hit upon a strategy for creating luminous interiors? The explanation may lie with his return to Europe in 1959 to attend the CIAM conference in Otterlo—the same year he began work on the First Unitarian Church. While in Europe, Kahn visited Le Corbusier's Notre Dame du Haut at Ronchamp, France. Having abandoned mainstream modern architecture for his own very personal direction, Kahn must have been curious about Ronchamp and the vitriolic condemnation it attracted from conservative modernist critics. Le Corbusier stood accused of architectural heresy for what some considered his gothic, retrograde church.

Kahn "fell madly in love"[7] with Ronchamp, and it is clear from the several sketches he made of the project that he thoroughly understood the sophisticated control of light.[8] Although he did not draw the light shafts at Ronchamp, they would not have escaped his attention. Only months after returning to the United States, Kahn developed the second proposal for the First Unitarian Church, which broke the rigid biaxial symmetry of the first and clustered the offices and supporting program around a central square hall. It can be no coincidence that in the process of reconfiguring the church, he incorporated light monitors that collect and diffuse light almost exactly as do those of Le Corbusier's Ronchamp.

The influence of Le Corbusier on Kahn's ideas about architecture cannot be in doubt. Kahn once mentioned that in the 1930s he had lived in a beautiful city called Corbusier.[9] Two years before he died, Kahn referred to inspiration he derived from Le Corbusier:

> *I often say to myself, "How'm I doing, Corbusier?" You see, Corbusier was my teacher . . . Paul Cret was my teacher, Corbusier was my teacher.*[10]

In 1965, only months before the death of Le Corbusier, Kahn permitted himself to fantasize about the light and form of some magnificent future work of Le Corbusier:

> *I believe that Le Corbusier, even in the light of his marvelous revelations about architecture, is just beginning to create his greatest work. I dare to think of a building he might make, a great block of a building, which is cut into from top to bottom in varied places of varied shapes . . . giving light to spaces and passages on the immediate interior and leading to a glorious central and single space, the walls and their light left in faceted planes, the shapes of the record of their making, intermingled with the serenity of light from above.*[11]

It was left to Kahn himself to explore this fantasy with the Hurva Synagogue, the Dacca Assembly Chamber, and the central hall of the Exeter library. After his visit to Ronchamp in 1959, Kahn was consistently able to find increasingly ingenious ways to create the most ethereal of ambient light and shadow in his interiors.

Kahn used what was probably the best tool available for visualizing light in his day: large interior study models lit by lamps to simulate the sun. That this worked for him is certain, but a review of the model photographs made by Kahn's office reveals that quite a leap of imagination is required to understand what would really happen with light in finished space. The models are schematic, lacking detail and delineation of materials. The light, in most cases, only begins to approximate what would occur in the built space, as is evident in a comparison to photographs of the completed projects. Today we can simulate the light Kahn loved with an accuracy unimaginable in his time. Would Kahn have made use of these tools in his design process had they been available? As his long-time associate Marshall Meyers said:

> *Who is to say? He was fascinated by technology and once said to me that Michelangelo would have used the light bulb had it been available.*[12]

Louis I. Kahn

Unbuilt Masterworks

U.S. Consulate

Luanda, Angola, 1959–61

The design of the U.S. Consulate in Luanda began a focused exploration of an idea that was to continue for the rest of Louis I. Kahn's career: the incorporation of unglazed, independent forms borrowed from the ruins of the ancient world into a very modernist architecture. Luanda is an important transitional project, falling between the Yale University Art Gallery, the Trenton bathhouse, and the Alfred Newton Richards Medical Research Building—where Kahn first began to find his architectural voice—and the Salk Institute and the First Unitarian Church at Rochester—where he turned the corner into full maturity as a master architect. An understanding of the evolution of Kahn's thinking about architecture as it relates to the architecture of the Old World helps put Luanda into context.

Beaux-Arts

The four years that Kahn spent at the University of Pennsylvania, from 1920 to 1924, coincided with the great architectural revolutions of the European avant-garde and the Russian constructivists. He entered college one year after Walter Gropius founded the Bauhaus in Germany and precisely as Le Corbusier's magazine *L'Esprit Nouveau* was at the height of its influence. Kahn, however, was somewhat insulated from these movements. He studied under an American variation of the French Beaux-Arts tradition as developed by one of the great teachers of that time, Paul Cret. By the time Kahn entered the University of Pennsylvania, Cret had developed the architectural program into the strongest in the United States. Kahn excelled in what Cret labeled "stripped classicism," or "modern classic"—an architecture with its roots in nineteenth-century classical architecture but simplified due to the influence of modernism. It bridged neoclassicism and twentieth-century modernism and encouraged a skewing and breaking of axes, which had become relentless and sterile in the nineteenth century. A clear expression of mass, load-bearing masonry walls, and deep openings was emphasized (figs. 5, 6). Drawing skills and an understanding of history were developed through freehand sketching and watercolor shade and shadow studies of great historic works.[1] All of this was to serve Kahn well thirty years later.

3 (preceding page). U.S. Consulate, Chancellery Building. View from offices to steps at entry.

4 (opposite). U.S. Consulate, Chancellery Building. View to offices beyond recessed entry.

5 (above). Monumental Fountain (student project), University of Pennsylvania, Philadelphia, School of Fine Arts, Architecture, c. 1924.

6 (overleaf). Office of John Molitor (Louis I. Kahn, illustrator). Perspective of main portico, Palace of Liberal Arts, Sesquicentennial International Exhibition, Philadelphia, Pennsylvania, 1925–26.

After graduating, Kahn spent five years working for Paul Cret and others, practicing the kind of architecture he had learned in school, with a one-year break to travel and sketch. During his first visit to the Old World, he produced beautiful pencil and watercolor studies of medieval and Renaissance structures, which eventually contributed to the vocabulary of forms and images he drew on twenty-five years later: the towers of San Gimignano and the hill towns of Italy (figs. 7–10). Through a Beaux-Arts concern for more literal representation, Kahn focused on communicating the mass and integrity of a structure, the play of light, and the rich textures of materials.

Modernism

Kahn returned from his travels in Europe in 1929 to find the architectural practices of Philadelphia withering after the stock market crash in October. That same year, Mies van der Rohe completed his Barcelona Pavilion and Le Corbusier began work on the Villa Savoye. A new architecture that could not be ignored was in the air. Kahn, and most of his under-employed colleagues, became converts to modernism, looking to Le Corbusier and the European avant-garde for inspiration, with the free plan, thin membrane enclosures, and sculptural gestures. He continued in this direction for the next twenty years, focusing primarily on single- and multifamily housing and producing architecture that was less than remarkable. Kahn would be a tiny footnote in the history of twentieth-century architecture if the work of this period were all that remained to assess him by. His architecture in the 1940s was a variation of the standardized International Style architecture of the time (fig. 11). Most striking about his work of this period is that it shows little of the intense passion found in his architecture of only a few years later. Vincent Scully wrote of Kahn's work at the time when they began to teach together at Yale in 1947:

He wasn't bad at it, but he wasn't exceptionally good at it either. And he would have not become the Kahn we know had he continued to do it either. He just didn't feel it.[2]

7 (opposite). Towers,
San Gimignano, Italy.
Watercolor on paper, 1929.

8 (top). Townscape, Positano, Italy.
Watercolor on paper, 1929.

9 (right). Coastal town,
Amalfi coast, Italy.
Watercolor on paper, 1929.

10 (far right). Coastal town,
Amalfi coast, Italy.
Watercolor on paper, 1929.

Scully also commented:

It was clear that here was a man who'd lost an order and was looking for it everywhere. What that order was nobody knew. He didn't know himself, but he constantly talked about it . . . it was as if he, like a lot of people in architecture and art history in the late forties, wanted to get outside art, to something that would sanction art.[3]

But there were hints of what was to come. In 1944, Kahn wrote an article called "On Monumentality" that described aspects of ancient monumental architecture he still found relevant, such as spiritual qualities of permanence, integrity of structure, and the possibilities of Roman forms:

Monumentality in architecture may be defined as a quality, a spiritual quality inherent in a structure which conveys the feeling of its eternity, that it cannot be added to or changed. We feel that quality in the Parthenon, the recognized architectural symbol of Greek Civilization . . . The influence of the Roman vault, the dome, the arch, has etched itself in deep furrows across the pages of architectural history . . . they will continue to reappear but with the added powers made possible by our technology.[4]

Clearly he had not entirely turned his back on the Beaux-Arts education he had received at the University of Pennsylvania. Neither had he found a way to bring this thinking into his own work.

11 (below). Triangle Redevelopment Project, Philadelphia, Pennsylvania, 1946–48. Perspective of Civic Center. Inscribed Louis I. Kahn '47.

12 (right). U.S. Consulate, Chancellery Building. View toward main entry.

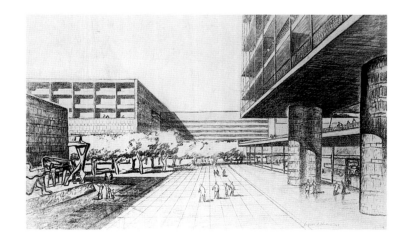

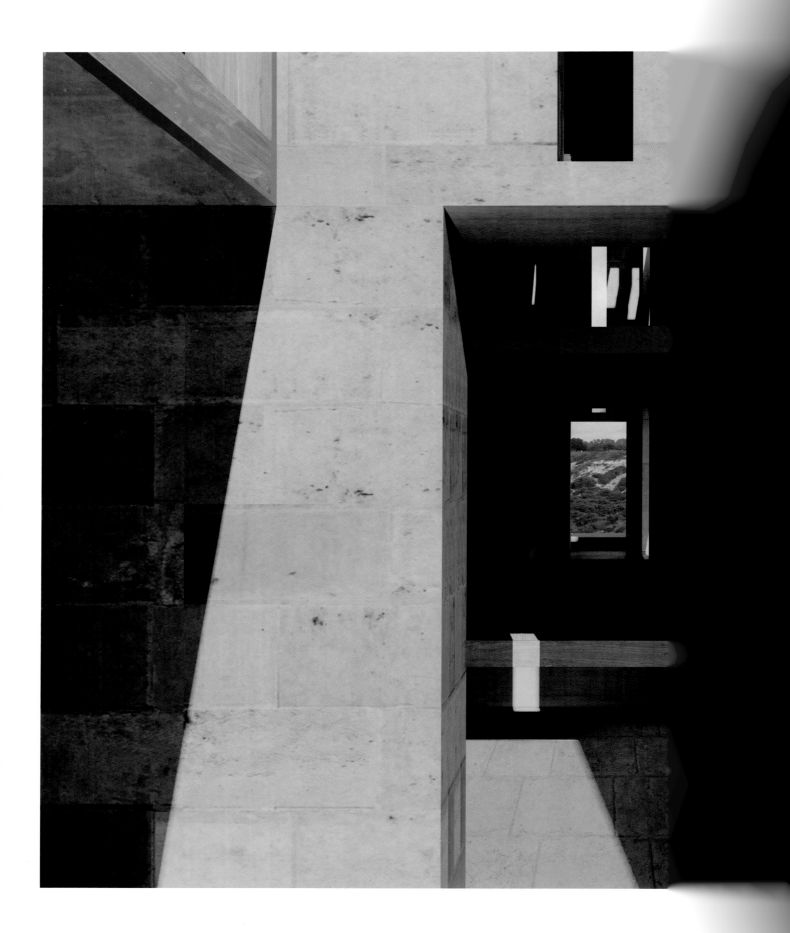

13. U.S. Consulate, Chancellery Building. View at exterior ambulatory.

The American Academy in Rome

In 1950, Kahn accepted an offer to become the architect in residence at the American Academy in Rome. Kahn, who turned fifty during the four months he spent at the Academy, was at this point in his life a respected teacher at Yale but hardly a major architect. At an age when most professionals are set in their ways with established careers, Kahn arrived in Rome already questioning the ideology of modernism that he had uncomfortably adopted twenty years earlier. Only days after arriving in Italy, Kahn wrote a letter to the members of his office expressing a desire to incorporate into his work what he was discovering in Italy:

I firmly realize that the architecture of Italy will remain as the inspirational source of the works of the future. Those who don't see it that way ought to look again. Our stuff looks tinny compared to it and all the pure forms that have been tried in all its variations . . . What is necessary is the interpretation of the architecture of Italy as it relates to our knowledge of building and needs. I care little for the restorations . . . but I see great personal value in reading (one's own approach) to the creation of space modified by the buildings around as a point of departure. I find it of little difficulty translating the masonry construction into steel and concrete and I intend to have the Fellows explore their reactions to what they see into similar aims. They are quite excited by the idea.[5]

Many of the elements in Kahn's mature work can be traced back to the experiences of these four months. Clearly it was a time of profound change for him. He spoke of the effect of this period in Rome to Michael Graves some years later, as Graves recalled in an interview:

He regretted wasting so much of his time trying to be a modern architect. He said, "Michael, I tried and tried all my life to make the wall thinner and thinner and thinner." It wasn't until he went to Rome . . . that he realized the strength of the wall, the power of chiaroscuro, the interest in light, and all of what architecture eventually held for him. He said he finally felt he was at home with architecture.[6]

14 (opposite). U.S. Consulate, Chancellery Building. View opposite main entrance.

15 (above). U.S. Consulate, Chancellery Building. View from offices.

In Rome, Kahn found a reflection of the order he was looking for in ancient ruins. He was led directly to a recognition of this order by one of the great classical archaeologists of the time, Frank E. Brown, also a fellow at the Academy. Kahn often attended the biweekly field trips led by Brown to the archaeological sites around Rome and had the great fortune of experiencing these ancient buildings under his influence. Kahn's sense of order, as it developed in Rome, was quite different from the symmetrical, geometrical order practiced by architects such as Edward Durell Stone and Minoru Yamasaki after World War II—too often an overly simplistic and decorative ordering of parts. To Kahn, order evolved to mean not just a geometric order but a kind of Platonic ideal discovered through a process of inquiry into roots and fundamentals—into archetypes. In the ancient world, Kahn found an architecture that was crafted specifically to accommodate ritual and human activity, as Frank Brown so eloquently discussed in his book *Roman Architecture*. Here were the pure forms and classical order that returned Kahn to his Beaux-Arts roots. Here were the ruins that eventually found their way into his work. Kahn discovered in Rome a fundamental concern with structure and the nature of materials. He found an ancient light that later infiltrated the interior of his buildings. But it took Kahn ten years to integrate these concerns fully.

Kahn and the architectural fellows of the Academy began a sketching tour of Egypt and Greece in January 1951. That Kahn's approach to architecture was changing dramatically can be seen in the contrast between his 1951 drawings and those of his first trip to Europe in the late 1920s. A concern for depicting mass, light, and basic form is evident throughout, but the later drawings are much less a descriptive representation of architecture. They are, in a sense, a bridge between Beaux-Arts classicism and a more primal and abstract modernism. Kahn selected the solid saturated colors of pastels over the more subtle medium of watercolors, which he had used so effectively on his first trip—but which had become a medium too strongly linked to the

Beaux-Arts and not sufficiently modernist for the Kahn of the 1950s. His mysterious charcoal sketch of the Temple of Amon at Luxor has the kind of complex layering of powerful elements we find in his architecture of the mid-1960s, as do the drawings of the three pyramids of Giza or the fragments of walls and columns of the Propylaea at the Acropolis in Athens (fig. 16–18).

Works of the 1950s

While at the American Academy, Kahn received word that he had been awarded the first major commission of his life, the Yale University Art Gallery. Experiencing this building today, the sense of Kahn's struggle to find a modernist expression for the lessons learned in Rome, Greece, and Egypt is quite apparent. Some have seen evidence of Kahn's well-known appreciation of the pyramids of Egypt, visited just months before, or the geodesics of Buckminster Fuller in the tetrahedrons of the gallery's ceiling. It is the powerful sense of mass and permanence, however, that can most directly be related to ancient architecture. The interior, with its exposed concrete and an almost threateningly heavy ceiling, reveals a definite link to the virility and weight of Roman ruins (fig. 21). This is the aspect of the building that most troubled many conventional modernists.

In plan and form, however, the gallery is fundamentally a Miesian universal loft, with movable partitions used to redefine space as required (fig. 22). In this sense the Yale Art Gallery was largely in keeping with the modernist traditions of the 1940s and 1950s. But there is in the art gallery a clear but tentative step away from the modernist ideal of continuity of space and toward the Roman ideal of "room space" specifically crafted to contain and support human activity. The concrete cylindrical stair Kahn placed within the center bay of the building is an independent enclosed volume defined by perfectly pure geometric forms (fig. 23). This is a world within a world, complete unto itself. It was later that Kahn first spoke of "wrapping ruins around buildings," with his U.S. Consulate at Luanda and Salk meeting

16 (top). Pyramids, Giza,
Egypt. Pastel on paper, 1951.

17 (above). Propylaea, Acropolis,
Athens, Greece.
Pastel on paper, 1951.

18 (opposite). Temple of Amon,
Luxor, Egypt. Charcoal on paper.
Inscribed Lou K '51.

19. U.S. Consulate, Chancellery
Building. View from offices.

house, but the stair at the Yale University Art Gallery is—if a reading that Kahn probably did not intend may be allowed—a separate ruin enclosed within a building.

Kahn was pleased with the success of this portion of the building and incorporated elements of it into later work. On the other hand, he was clearly unhappy with the universal and reconfigurable space he created for the gallery. Although highly acclaimed at the time, Kahn later admitted that he "failed to command the forces which could have produced a truly significant building."[7] In one talk he commented:

If I were to build a gallery now, I would really be more concerned about building spaces which are not used freely by the director as he wants. Rather I would give him spaces that were there and had certain characteristics.[8]

On the same theme, he noted, "A good building is one which the client cannot destroy by wrong use of space."[9]

Gradually the configuration of space in Kahn's architecture after 1951 took on more definite qualities of Roman space. In 1955, two years after completing the gallery, Kahn was retained to build a tiny project that he considered the turning point in his approach to architecture—the bathhouse at the Trenton Jewish Community Center (fig. 24). For the first time since returning from Rome in 1951, Kahn was able to build a project in which each function was contained in a discrete volume of space. This was as formally uncompromised and pure as any of the great basilicas of Rome—even if it was only a small, inexpensive structure built of concrete block and wood. Speaking of the project he was to develop three years after the bathhouse, Kahn said:

If the world discovered me after I designed the Richards towers building, I discovered myself after designing that little concrete-block bathhouse in Trenton.[10]

Kahn's next significant project was the Richards Medical Research Building at the

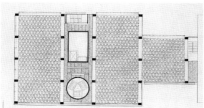

20 (opposite). U.S. Consulate, Chancellery Building. View from offices.

21 (top). Yale University Art Gallery, New Haven, Connecticut, 1951–53. View from gallery toward stair enclosure.

22 (above left). Yale University Art Gallery. Reflected ceiling plan.

23 (above right). Yale University Art Gallery. View to ceiling of stairway cylinder.

University of Pennsylvania of 1957–60, which brought him fully onto the international scene. Kahn extended the idea of defining visible, individual forms for separate functions by creating massive masonry exhaust and air-intake towers wrapped around glazed laboratories and studios (fig. 25). These towers have an uncanny resemblance to those of San Gimignano as sketched by Kahn in 1929. The brick towers, separate, uninhabited, and without glass, can be read as ancient monoliths surrounding the inhabited forms.

The Chancellery

In 1959, Kahn received the commission to design the U.S. Consulate in Luanda, Angola. He signed his agreement in December of that year and traveled to Angola to inspect the site in January 1960. The State Department required that each embassy building visibly reflect local conditions. Kahn took this to heart and attempted to develop a building that reflected in a fundamental way the harsh conditions of the Angolan desert.

The plan of the Chancellery Building (figs. 27, 28) appears, at first reading, unremarkable and banal. It is simple and rectangular, with perfect axial symmetry, except where minor compromises were necessary to satisfy the program. The main entrance is recessed in typical Beaux-Arts fashion, containing what appears to be a monumental stair. An arcade of sorts runs along both the north and south facades, and turns at each corner, only to be interrupted by projecting offices. The parti is much like a double-sided but less interesting version of the Kimbell Art Museum plan, which shows a similar axial symmetry, recessed entry, and arcade (fig. 29). Opposite the main entrance is an identical recess, but without stair, doors, or obvious purpose. The elevations and section show the same rigid symmetry (figs. 32, 33).

A closer examination of the plan reveals features that are more interesting. It hints of four carefully delineated sets of elements: sixteen identical detached wall segments (drawn without poché) are located at the east and west facades and on either side of the entry recesses; large panels of glass set in heavy frames face these detached walls; two thicker, unbroken walls (drawn with poché) are located on the north and south facades, with similar walls on the east and west facades; four pairs of rectangular columns (drawn with heavy poché) appear to be designed to support massive loads. In addition, the section and elevations reveal a baffling second structure that floats above the roof and is supported by four massive girders.

Ruins Wrapped around Buildings

The organizing principle of the building becomes clear in Kahn's discussion of the project. Kahn spoke in detail about this idea in a 1961 interview:

I am doing a building in Africa, which is very close to the equator. The glare is killing. Everybody looks black against the sunlight. Light is a needed thing, but still an enemy . . . When you were in the interior of any building, looking at a window was unbearable because of the glare. The dark walls framing the brilliant light outside made you very uncomfortable. The tendency was to look away from the window . . . I thought, wouldn't it be good if one could find . . . an architectural expression for the problems of glare without adding devices to a window . . . which tells the story of the problems of glare.

I noticed that when people worked in the sun, they usually faced the wall and not the open country. Indoors, they would turn their chair towards the wall; the wall then becomes part of the window. Now, placing a wall in front of a window would cut the view and that is not pleasant . . . So I thought of putting openings in the wall . . . when the wall got the light—even direct sunlight—it would modify the glare.

So therefore I thought of the beauty of ruins . . . of things which nothing lives behind . . . and so I thought of wrapping ruins around buildings; you might say encasing a building in a ruin so that you look through the wall which has its apertures as if by accident . . . I felt this would be an answer to the glare problem.[11]

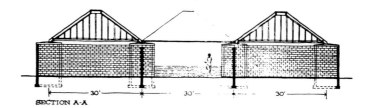

SECTION A-A

24 (opposite top). Bathhouse, Jewish Community
Center, Ewing Township (near Trenton), New Jersey,
c. 1957. Roof plan and section.

25 (opposite bottom). Richards Medical Research
Building, University of Pennsylvania, Philadelphia,
1957–60. View of entrance.

26 (above). U.S. Consulate, Chancellery Building.
View from offices.

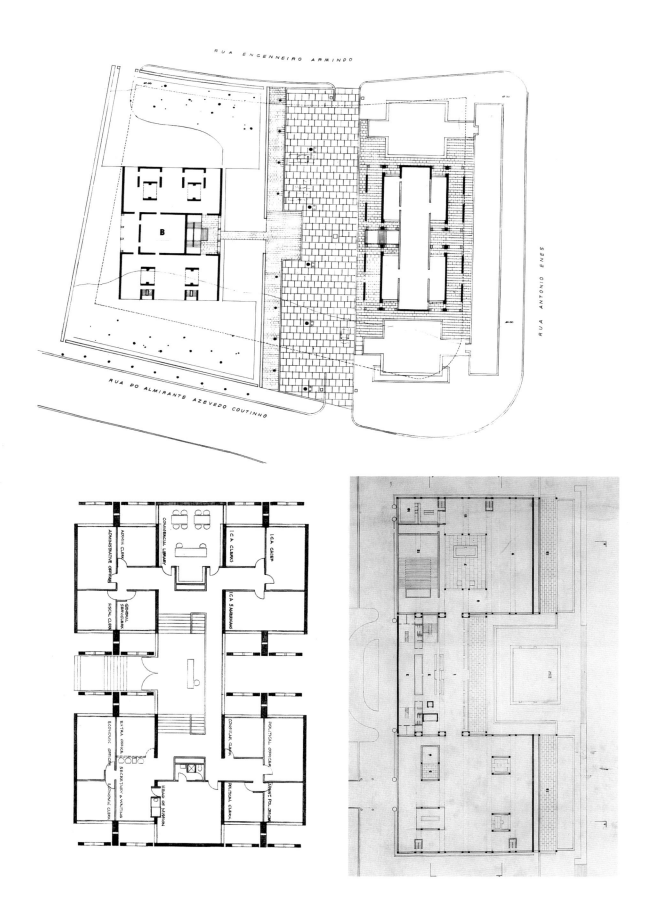

Thus the sixteen detached wall segments are the "ruins" wrapped around the building, which is enclosed by the lighter poché walls and glass panels. After observing that African people who worked outdoors often faced the wall of a building and its soft reflected light rather than the glare of the open arid country, Kahn devised a strategy to simulate this effect by placing "ruins" with unglazed openings at the east and west facades, some eight feet beyond the large windows of the chancellery offices. Cut into these planes are keyhole arched openings, variations of those used at the Tribune Review Publishing Company Building, begun two years before the start of Luanda, and at the unbuilt Fleisher house of the same year. While the impulse to use unglazed forms related to the ruins of Rome was no doubt aesthetic, the rationale was to control glare. Kahn intended light to enter this intermediate exterior zone between building and "ruin," where it would reflect, soften, and scatter. Between black and white, this gray zone would allow the eyes to make a comfortable transition from the relatively dark interior to the brilliant light of the arid land beyond.

Sun Roof/Rain Roof

An isometric of an exterior corner showing the relationship of all four sets of elements and a partial section and elevation of the east and west wall conditions are descriptive enough to allow the entire building to be assembled through extrapolation (figs. 35, 37). The massive rectangular columns, distinguished from the enclosing walls by their construction with a smaller stone module, are paired to support the four concrete girders, which in turn support regular beams and U-shaped sun fins. This secondary structure is entirely independent of the roof membrane. Kahn described the traditional African architecture that inspired this roof structure:

I saw some buildings that were conscious of the heat generated by roofs . . . They had large separations between ceiling and roof . . . small openings which were visible from the outside in which

27 (opposite top). U.S. Consulate, Chancellery Building and Residence. Site plan. Dated 30 Aug 1960.

28 (opposite bottom left). U.S. Consulate, Chancellery Building. Upper-level plan. Dated 30 Sept 1960.

29 (opposite bottom right). Kimbell Art Museum, Fort Worth, Texas, 1966–72. First-floor plan. Undated, c. fall 1968.

30 (above). U.S. Consulate, Chancellery Building. Exterior view of "ruin walls."

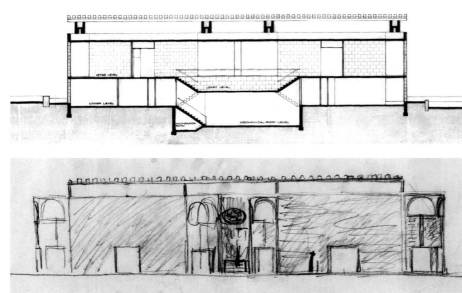

a breeze could come in to ventilate the areas in the ceiling and roof plane. And I thought how wonderful it would be if one could separate the sun problems from the rain problems. And it came to mind to have a sun roof purely for the sun and another roof purely for the rain. I placed them six feet away from each other so that one could maintain the rain roof . . . the actual sun roof might become the insulation so I would eliminate insulation on the rain roof entirely.[12]

Perhaps aware that the complex sun roof would cost far more than the most sophisticated insulation system, Kahn was searching for a way to express clearly, in architectural form, his concern for the severe environmental problems caused by a climate like Luanda's. Kahn criticized the type of sunscreen devices used by Edward Durell Stone as creating little diamond points of glare against the dark ribs of the grillwork. To Kahn, this was a "department store" solution that was not integral to the architecture:

I felt that in bringing the rain roof and the sun roof away from each other, I was telling the man on the street his way of life. I was explaining the atmospheric conditions of wind, the conditions of light, the conditions of sun and glare to him. If I use a device—a clever kind of device—it would only seem like a design to him—something pretty. I didn't want anything pretty. I wanted to have a clear statement of a way of life . . . These are really crude statements . . . they should be primitively stated first rather than in a high degree of taste.[13]

For Luanda, Kahn managed to create a complex layering of elements clearly evident when experienced in perspective (figs. 39, 40) but not readily apparent in plan and section. Most interesting is the zone between "ruin" and building, where the light filtering through the sun roof above creates endless variations of shadow and highlights, as if through the leaves of a Tuscan grape arbor.

The project is also interesting for what it is not. As in the Yale University Art Gallery, Kahn is not yet defining space as discrete volumes. Although the control of light and glare is the central concern generating form, Kahn is not creating the kind of luminous light typical of most of his work after Luanda. Brightening the interior with light from above to reduce the contrast in lighting level between the interior and exterior may have been just as effective in moderating glare as his ruin walls. And although this is his first conscious attempt to wrap ruins around buildings, the ruin in this case is not yet the complex form that he was to develop in subsequent projects—as he confesses when comparing Luanda to his Indian Institute of Management in Ahmedabad:

In the school building, you notice that I introduced a light well. I think it is somewhat superior to the device I invented for Luanda, because there I put a wall up to shade the sun and modify the glare, and here the solution is an integral part. The construction of the building is better as well because . . . the windows are not on the exterior where you don't want them.[14]

Ultimately, the bureaucrats at the State Department found Kahn's sun roof "bizarre" and his strategy for controlling glare "rather cold and formidable."[15] When the project was canceled in August 1961, Kahn was already immersed in the design of the meeting house of the Salk Institute—a more sophisticated elaboration of ideas first explored in Luanda.

31 (opposite top). U.S. Consulate, Chancellery Building. Interior view from offices.

32 (opposite middle). U.S. Consulate, Chancellery Building. Longitudinal section. Dated 30 Sept 1960.

33 (opposite bottom). U.S. Consulate, Chancellery Building. Sketch of exterior elevation. Undated, c. 1960.

34 (above). U.S. Consulate, Chancellery Building. View of roof structure.

35 (right). U.S. Consulate, Chancellery Building. Isometric drawing of wall and roof structure. Undated, fall 1960.

36 (opposite top). U.S. Consulate, Chancellery Building. View of zone between glazing and "ruin wall."

37 (opposite bottom). U.S. Consulate, Chancellery Building. Section and elevation of zone between glazing and "ruin wall." Undated, fall 1960.

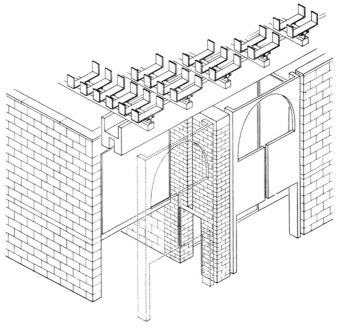

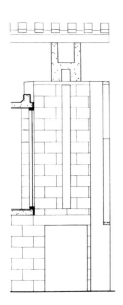

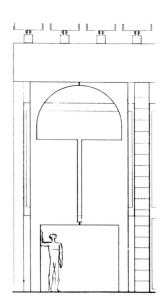

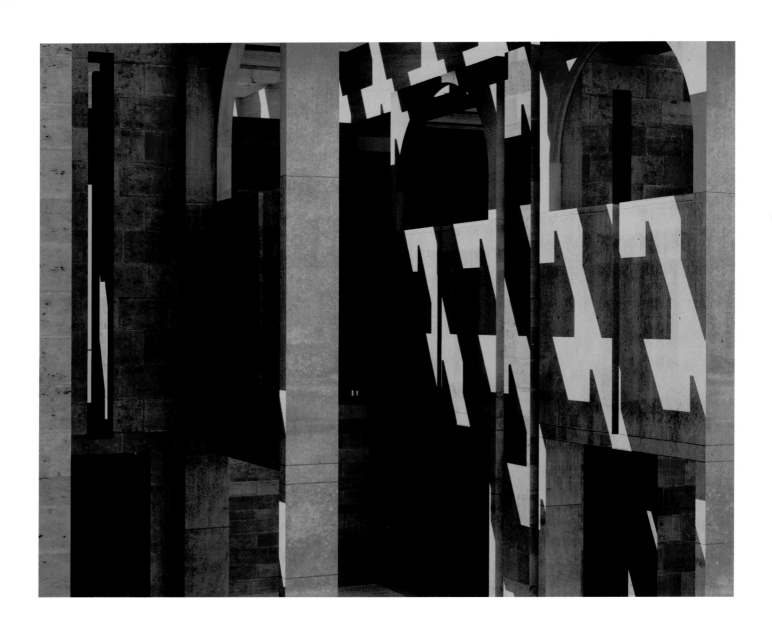

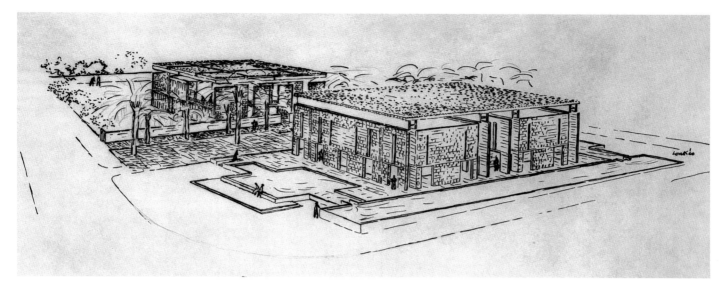

38 (opposite). U.S. Consulate, Chancellery Building. Exterior view opposite entrance.

39 (top). U.S. Consulate, Chancellery Building and Residence. Aerial perspective. Ink and graphite on white trace. Undated, 1960.

40 (above left). U.S. Consulate, Chancellery Building and Residence. Ink and graphite on white trace. Inscribed Lou K '60.

41 (above right). U.S. Consulate, Chancellery Building. Isometric of exterior corner.

Meeting House
of the Salk Institute

La Jolla, California, 1959–65

Jonas Salk envisioned the Salk Institute for Biological Studies as a place where artists and humanists could inform and inspire those working on the frontiers of science. He found in Kahn a collaborator who could give architectural form to this desire. The commitment was written into the mission statement of the institute, but better evidence can be found in the list of humanist scholars invited to La Jolla—a list headed by Jacob Bronowski. Best known for his passionate and eloquent presentation of the ethical and humanistic aspects of science in the 1973 "Ascent of Man" series for the BBC, Bronowski was a resident fellow of the Salk Institute from its opening until his death in 1974.

Humanism and Science

Sadly for Dr. Bronowski and his colleagues, only the scientific component of Kahn's vision was built. The other two facilities, the meeting house and the houses for the fellows, were never realized. It does not detract from the laboratory's status as one of the masterworks of twentieth-century architecture to point out that it was the meeting house that most interested Kahn in the early phases of the project (fig. 43). In 1960, long before the Salk Institute design had assumed its final form, Kahn's preoccupation with the meeting house was evident, and he spoke of the laboratories almost as an afterthought:

I had been asked to be the architect for the academy of biology in San Diego. I had no program whatsoever. What do you think the building should be like? I said . . . there would be fine, generous spaces which need not be all named for their purposes, just wonderful spaces to come to. It would certainly have places of meeting. There would be places of dining . . . places where people could stay overnight, gymnasium, swimming pool, arcades, seminar rooms, and so on. One would say: Where are the laboratories? We are talking about laboratories too. Essentially it is a laboratory building, but you must not forget that the place of meeting is almost of major importance.[1]

42 (preceding page). Meeting House of the Salk Institute. Exterior view from the "quiet fountain" court toward the residence.

43 (opposite). Meeting House of the Salk Institute. Sketches, undated.

44 (above). Meeting House of the Salk Institute. Exterior view looking toward the seminary rooms.

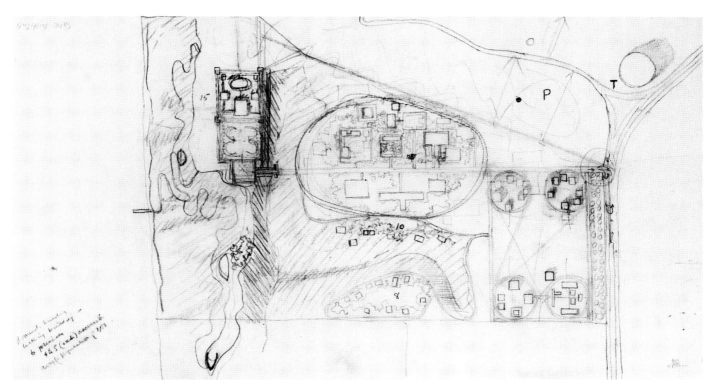

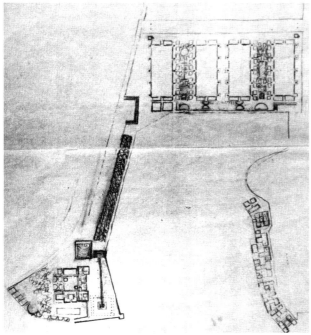

45 (opposite). Meeting House of the Salk Institute. Exterior view from the "quiet fountain" court toward the residence and seminary rooms.

46 (top). Meeting House of the Salk Institute. Site plan sketch of first phase. Undated, c. January 1960.

47 (above). Meeting House of the Salk Institute. Site plan sketch of second phase.

The laboratories were built for work, while the meeting house was the humanist soul of the institute. Salk said of his first meeting with Kahn:

I spoke about the desirability of creating a place where not only scientists would be comfortable, but artists—and I used the notion of a place to which I would like to invite Picasso.[2]

The meeting house is where Picasso may have discussed art and life with Bronowski after a tour of the laboratories. Placed away from the laboratories on the edge of a bluff overlooking the Pacific Ocean, it would have been a retreat for quiet reflection and personal study as well as a place to exercise, share meals, and attend concerts, lectures, and seminars.

The Salk Master Plan

The initial proposal for the Salk was developed in the spring of 1960 (fig. 46). At this point, there were seven distinct components to the project, in keeping with Kahn's insistence on separate forms to house separate and distinct activities: two laboratory groupings on circular bases set inland, two service buildings adjacent to the laboratories, the meeting house at the far end of the site near the steep bluff descending to the Pacific, a cluster of recreational buildings placed along the drive linking the laboratories to the meeting house, and a group of residential structures located across the ravine from the recreational component. This was "an early fantasy" that was soon revised.[3]

One year later, the project had assumed the final basic arrangement. Working without a detailed program, Kahn defined three independent components. The laboratories, still inland, had two plazas instead of the final one, and the residences stayed near their original location (fig. 47). The meeting house was moved inland, near the area formerly occupied by the recreation buildings, and became a series of discrete clustered volumes (fig. 48).

Meeting House

The contrast between the meeting house and the laboratory could not be more distinct. The laboratory plaza is a cosmic void defined by scaleless concrete planes. It is broken only by a single line of water, as at the Alhambra, and links the vast heartland of America to the greatest expanse in the world—the Pacific Ocean. This pure and perfect statement of a simple and powerful idea creates what is perhaps the most sublime space of the twentieth century (fig. 54).

The meeting house, on the other hand, is almost picturesque (figs. 52, 77). It appears as a memory of some medieval monastery, or a village on the Amalfi coast of Italy (see figs. 9, 10), or perhaps surviving fragments of an ancient ruin. It is, in a very real sense, all of these. Kahn had a keen memory and visual intelligence and mentally catalogued all that interested him to draw on when needed. He often spoke of ancient works as a source of inspiration but—always the modern architect who sought pure, fresh creation—rarely acknowledged any literal borrowing from the past. Yet history can be felt in all of Kahn's best work. Kahn read little, but consumed drawings and photographs. Piranesi's imagined reconstruction

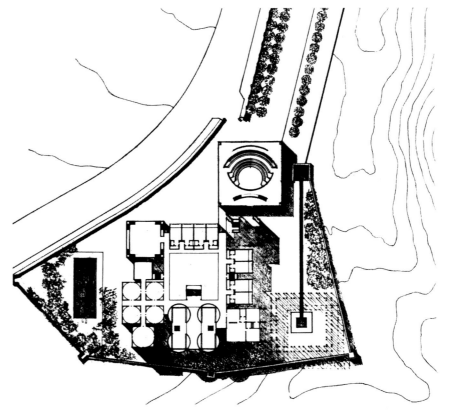

48 (top). Meeting House of the Salk Institute. Plan. Undated, c. April 1961.

49 (above left). Meeting House of the Salk Institute. View of zone between dining room and "ruin wall."

50 (above right). Meeting House of the Salk Institute. View of zone between seminary room and "ruin wall."

51 (opposite). Meeting House of the Salk Institute. View of zone between dining room and "ruin wall."

52 (above). Meeting House of the Salk Institute. Aerial perspective with unbuilt meeting house in foreground and built laboratories at upper left. Undated, c. 1962.

53 (left). Meeting House of the Salk Institute. Exterior view toward residence and library reading room.

54 (opposite). Salk Institute for Biological Studies, La Jolla, California, 1959–65. View of laboratory courtyard.

of the Campus Martius in Rome hung above his desk in Philadelphia, and many have identified fragments of Kahn's built work in this drawing.

Not surprisingly, several historical precedents for the forms of the meeting house can be clearly identified. Early in the design process, Salk himself suggested that the northern Italian monastery at Assisi had the architectural character he was seeking to create. Kahn knew this work well, having sketched it during his European trip of 1929. In a letter to the historian William H. Jordy in mid-1960, Kahn wrote that he hoped to travel to Italy "to see again the wonderful monasteries which have a bearing on what I am doing for Mr. Salk in San Diego."[4] It is perhaps the arcades, courtyard, and complex arrangement of the meeting house that can be most closely linked to Assisi, however different the forms.

55 (above left). Meeting House of the Salk Institute. View from zone between dining room and "ruin wall" looking north toward pool.

56 (above right). Meeting House of the Salk Institute. View from the seminary room looking west toward the Pacific Ocean.

57 (opposite). Meeting House of the Salk Institute. View from zone between dining room and "ruin wall" looking west toward the Pacific Ocean.

The plan owes much to Hadrian's Villa, as first reported by Vincent Scully in his 1962 book on Kahn:

Patterns from Rome and, most particularly, from Ancient Rome as imagined by Piranesi at the very beginning of the modern age, have played a part in the process at the Meeting House as well. (An early sketch had been traced by a draftsman, partly as a joke, from a plan of one of the units of Hadrian's Villa itself). "That's it," said Kahn.[5]

Kahn did not appreciate the publication of this reference, but it was confirmed in 1990 by the draftsman to whom Scully refers, architect Thomas Vreeland. Vreeland's site plan with the sketch of Hadrian's Villa is in the Louis I. Kahn Collection at the University of Pennsylvania[6] (fig. 61).

The early design for the meeting house was a rigid rectilinear building sitting uncomfortably on the irregular site, but it quickly began to evolve toward its final form. Grouped around a central multipurpose hall were the library, dining rooms, lecture hall, gymnasium, and apartments for the director and visitors—each with a unique form. A five-hundred-seat amphitheater was located on the inland side, with a nearby "noisy fountain" linked to a "quiet fountain" by way of the same Alhambra-like slit of water centered in the laboratory plaza (fig. 60). The design of this large complex ended midway through the design development phase. The elements facing the water were far more developed than those facing the laboratory, with dimensioned details, wall sections, and elevations, even though they are incomplete and uncoordinated (figs. 64–66). It is evident that this is the area that most interested Kahn, and this is where the meeting house became a ruin.

58 (above). Meeting House of the Salk Institute. View looking southwest toward "quiet fountain" court.

59 (opposite). Meeting House of the Salk Institute. View from terrace outside of residence looking north.

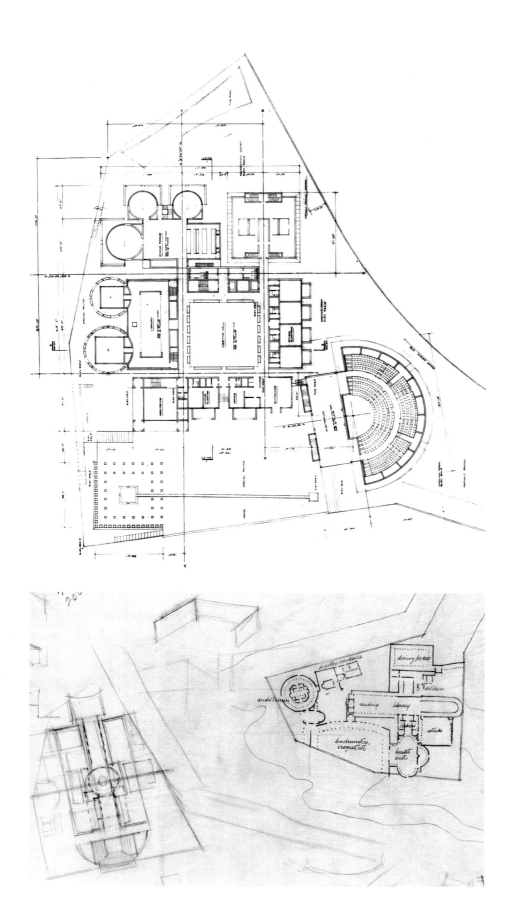

60 (above). Meeting House of the Salk Institute. First-floor plan, drawing number MH-A3. Inscribed January 17, 1962, revised 23 February 1962.

61 (left). Meeting House of the Salk Institute. Site plan with partial plan of Hadrian's Villa. Undated, 1960.

62 (opposite). Meeting House of the Salk Institute. View from first seminary room looking north toward second seminary room.

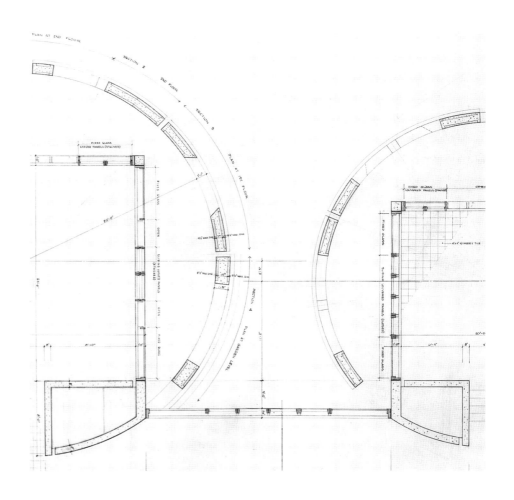

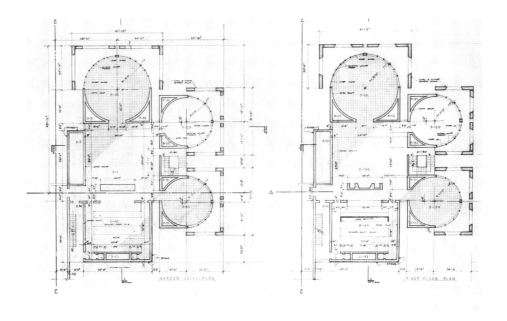

63 (opposite). Meeting House of the Salk Institute. View from zone between seminary room and "ruin wall" looking south.

64 (above). Meeting House of the Salk Institute. Plan detail of screen walls, drawing number MH-A205. Inscribed January 17, 1962, revised February 29, 1962.

65 (right). Meeting House of the Salk Institute. Garden-level and first-floor dining-room plans, drawing number MH-A301. Inscribed January 17, 1962, revised 28 February 1962.

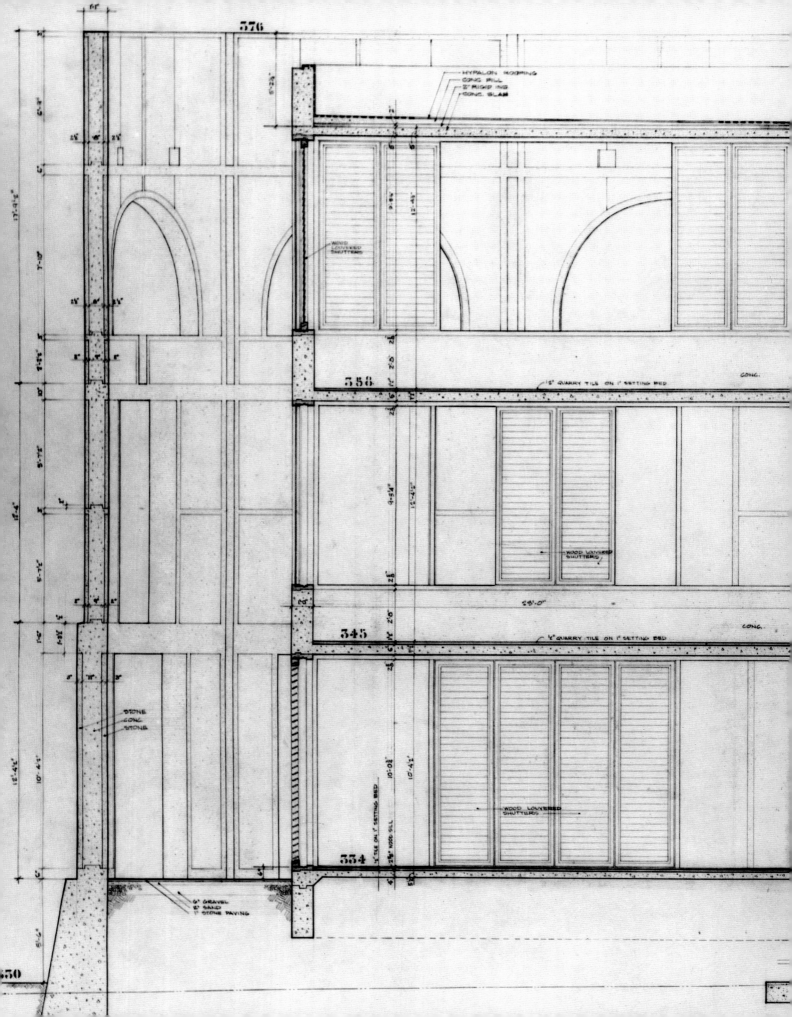

The Ruins of the Salk

The ruins at the U.S. Consulate at Luanda are strategically placed planes, while those of the Salk meeting house are much more Roman: three-dimensional, complete forms that define and enclose space. Although Kahn spoke of Luanda as "ruins wrapped around buildings," it was at the Salk that he truly accomplished this: fully exterior and independent cylindrical ruins wrap around cubic inhabitable space, and cubic ruins wrap around cylindrical inhabited space. These are the perfect geometries of square within circle and circle within square, repeated thousands of time from Vitruvius through the Middle Ages and the Renaissance. This geometry is present in Kahn's Trenton bathhouse, as well as at the Salk. As at Luanda, Kahn justifies the ruins of the Salk as devices to control glare. In April 1961, a sketch by Kahn appeared in *Progressive Architecture* diagramming precisely how the ruins of the Salk were conceived (fig. 72). He notes that "a glass wall needs protection from glare" and labels the Salk configurations "Architectural Solutions of Spaces Facing the Problems of Glare." Kahn said of this portion of the meeting house:

In the Salk project again, I am developing walls around buildings to take care of the glare . . . The architect must find an architecture out of glare, out of the wind, from which these shapes and dimensions are derived. And these glare walls are based on a very simple principle, which I got out of observation when I was in Africa, where the sun is startling . . . These walls I am developing for the Salk Center in San Diego are in recognition of this discovery of the laws of light, from which I have made a rule for myself in the design of the building.[7]

But as at Luanda, this system of double forms was not simply a device to control glare. It brought together the classical order of the great Roman ruins with a taut, thin, very modernist shell. These surrounding forms were the essence of the ruin—shapes without glass "which nothing lives behind." Again as with Luanda, it is not the interior space that is particularly interesting but the space between building and ruin.

66 (opposite). Meeting House of the Salk Institute. Library and seminary-room wall sections, drawing number MH-A204. Inscribed January 17, 1962, revised February 24, 1962.

67 (above) Meeting House of the Salk Institute. View from library looking west toward the Pacific Ocean.

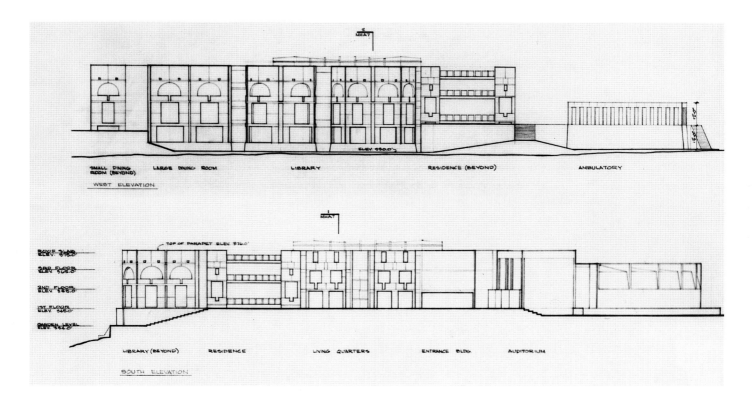

West elevation labels: SMALL DINING ROOM (BEYOND) — LARGE DINING ROOM — LIBRARY — RESIDENCE (BEYOND) — AMBULATORY

WEST ELEVATION

South elevation labels: LIBRARY (BEYOND) — RESIDENCE — LIVING QUARTERS — ENTRANCE BLDG. — AUDITORIUM

SOUTH ELEVATION

68 (opposite). Meeting House of the Salk Institute. View from zone between dining room and "ruin wall" looking west.

69 (top left). Meeting House of the Salk Institute. Detail of view from zone between dining room and "ruin wall" looking west.

70 (top right). Meeting House of the Salk Institute. Model built for the exhibition "Louis I. Kahn: In the Realm of Architecture," 1992–94.

71 (above). Meeting House of the Salk Institute. West and south elevations, drawing number MH-A9. Inscribed January 17, 1962, revised January 24, 1962.

In 1962, Kahn's office developed a schematic scale model of the meeting house, and Kahn made many sketches of the portion of the building facing the Pacific Ocean (figs. 71, 73). It is easy to imagine these forms cast in the same concrete Kahn used for the laboratories, or in the beautiful board-formed concrete of the Yale Art Gallery cylinder (see figs. 21, 22), or the finer cast-stone finish of the Yale Center for British Art stair cylinder. But the Salk drawings show an elaborate detail of concrete with recesses to accommodate thin sheets of stone veneer. The effect is that of a very thin concrete frame holding infill stone. Vincent Scully has written that since Salk

felt that stone would be much more soothing to the eye than concrete, Kahn sheathed them (and they will remain so at Salk's request if the money holds out) in soft yellow-brown Cordova sandstone from Texas, full of fossil crustaceans and more ambiguous biological life forms.[8]

The money, of course, did not hold out. There can be little doubt that had the meeting house been built, the stone would have been abandoned for concrete. Salk halted design work on the meeting house in 1963 as cost realities became clear. By 1965, $16 million had been spent on construction and fees, with the laboratory still an incomplete and unoccupied shell. The laboratories were slowly finished over the next few years as additional funds were raised, with the meeting house and residences, as Salk put it, "neither denied or dismissed."[9]

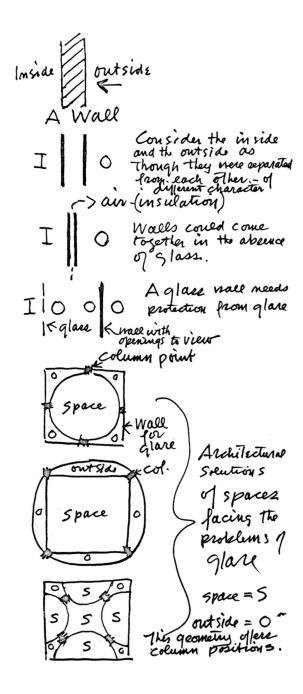

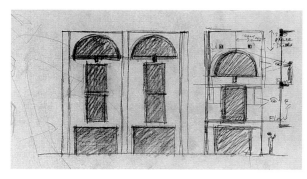

72 (opposite top). Meeting House of the Salk Institute. Diagrams for wall concept labeled "Architectural Solutions of Spaces Facing the Problems of Glare" as published in *Progressive Architecture*, April 1961.

73 (opposite bottom). Meeting House of the Salk Institute. Exterior elevation study, undated.

74 (above). Meeting House of the Salk Institute. View from first seminary room looking southeast toward residence.

75 (below). Meeting House of the
Salk Institute. View from second level
of residence terrace looking toward
first seminary room.

76 (opposite). Meeting House of the
Salk Institute. View from upper level
of residence terrace looking west
toward the Pacific Ocean.

77 (above). Meeting House of the
Salk Institute. Exterior perspective
sketch from the living place
(the village). Undated, 1962.

78 (opposite). Meeting House of the
Salk Institute. View between dining
rooms looking north toward pool.

79 (opposite). Meeting House of the Salk Institute. View from lower level of residence terrace looking southwest toward built laboratories.

80 (above left). Meeting House of the Salk Institute. View from second level of residence terrace looking west toward the Pacific Ocean.

81 (above right). Meeting House of the Salk Institute. View from residence terrace looking south toward "quiet fountain" court.

Mikveh Israel Synagogue

Philadelphia, Pennsylvania, 1961–72

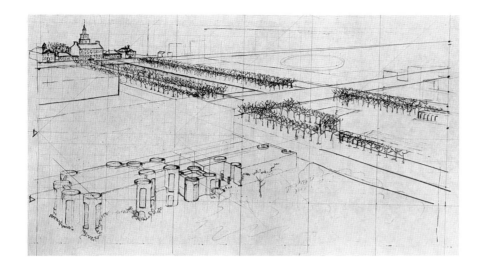

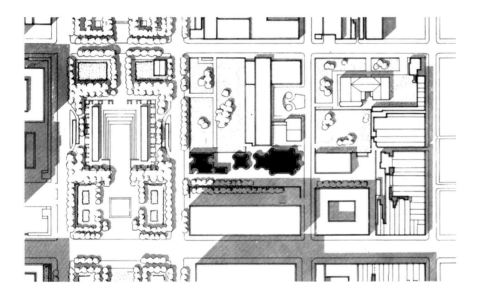

82 (preceding page). Mikveh Israel Synagogue. View from tower at entry lobby toward sanctuary.

83 (opposite). Mikveh Israel Synagogue. View from women's seating area toward entry.

84 (top). Mikveh Israel Synagogue. Aerial perspective of site, with synagogue at lower left and Independence Hall at upper left, c. 1965.

85 (above). Mikveh Israel Synagogue. Site plan with synagogue at center and Independence Mall at left. Undated, 1966.

Sue Ann Kahn recalls that her father's greatest professional disappointment was probably his inability to build the Mikveh Israel Synagogue.[1] Not only was this Louis Kahn's first opportunity to build a great religious space, but it was to be located in his hometown of Philadelphia. Mikveh Israel is one of Kahn's richest and most complex designs, which is to say, one of the most interesting of the twentieth century. There are many ways to view Mikveh: the accommodation to Jewish ritual; the link to Jewish mysticism; the expression of Kahn's often repeated theme of ruins wrapped around buildings; the forms borrowed from history; the subtle manipulation of light and space; and the role this work played in the evolution of Kahn's ideas about architecture.

In 1963, Richard Meier organized an exhibition at the Jewish Museum in New York City called "Recent American Synagogue Architecture." Included were designs by architects such as Marcel Breuer, Frank Lloyd Wright, Philip Johnson, Eric Mendelsohn, Minoru Yamasaki, and Kahn. At the time, Meier wrote that Kahn's Mikveh Israel was the "most important synagogue project of recent years." Twenty-three years later at the same museum, Meier, Paul Goldberger, and Vincent Scully discussed Kahn's unbuilt synagogue works. It was agreed that Mikveh Israel was perhaps the greatest synagogue design of modern architecture. It is a great loss that Kahn, one of the most prominent Jewish architects of the twentieth century, left this and his other monumental synagogue, the Hurva, unbuilt.

Kahn began the project in May 1961. The U.S. Consulate project in Angola was coming to an end, and the design of the Salk Institute was well underway. Kahn was hired by a Sephardic congregation who wished to return to historic Philadelphia, where they had built their first synagogue in 1822. Kahn helped them select a site adjacent to Independence Mall, with a central axis terminating in Independence Hall (figs. 84, 85). The congregation did not at the time have sufficient resources to build a new structure but hoped that a successful fund-raising campaign could be developed.

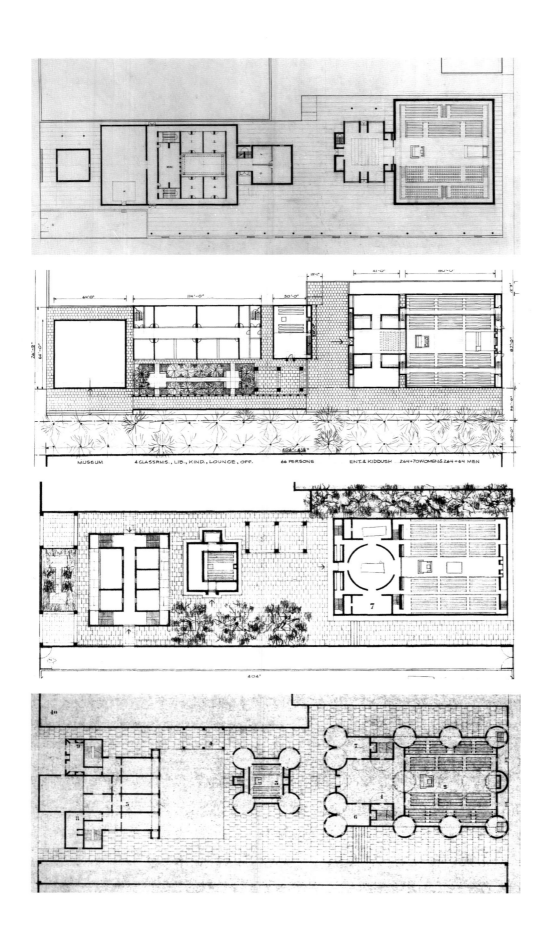

86 (top). Mikveh Israel Synagogue. First-floor plan. Dated "before April '62."

87 (second from top). Mikveh Israel Synagogue. First-floor plan. Dated 10 April 1962, revised 1 May 1962.

88 (third from top). Mikveh Israel Synagogue. First-floor plan, proposal with circular lobby. Dated 22 June 1962.

89 (left). Mikveh Israel Synagogue. First-floor plan, proposal with towers. Dated 14 August 1962.

90 (opposite). Mikveh Israel Synagogue. View from tower to tower.

Mikveh Israel was to be in the Orthodox tradition of Spain, where the Sephardic Jews originated before they were expelled during the time of the Inquisition. This tradition requires a central seating area for men, separate screened areas for women, a bema in the center from which the Torah is read, and an ark to house the valuable scrolls at the eastern end of the space. The Sephardic synagogue must serve as house of study, house of prayer, and house of community. The fundamental problem in Orthodox synagogue design is the requirement that the facility comfortably house the more intimate services of a typical Saturday, the large crowds of the High Holy Days, and social functions. Kahn recognized that most synagogue designs failed by attempting to accommodate, in a single space, these quite separate functions. He insisted that spaces be crafted to contain and reinforce each unique activity. In particular, a clear separation of the sacred from the secular—essential to Kahn's deeply held ideas about architecture—set the project on a course that produced a design of great depth and artistry—but a design that a congregation of limited means ultimately could not support.

Kahn quickly established a basic organization of the project with his first formal proposal of April 1962, featuring three distinct spaces for study, prayer, and community (fig. 86). Two variations of this proposal quickly followed in May and June (figs. 87, 88). Later in 1962, the essential element of Mikveh Israel had been incorporated into the design: "window rooms" that surround the sanctuary (fig. 89). This proposal was followed by the octagonal arrangement of eight cylinders enclosing an octagonal sanctuary, dated October 23, 1962 (fig. 92). The congregation voted to approve the design despite the $2.25 million estimated cost and a report by the treasurer that the building fund had only $231,000 and unwritten pledges of an additional $100,000.[2] The October 23 plan defined the fundamental design that was refined over the next several years, leading to perhaps the definitive state of the design, dated October 29, 1963 (fig. 91).

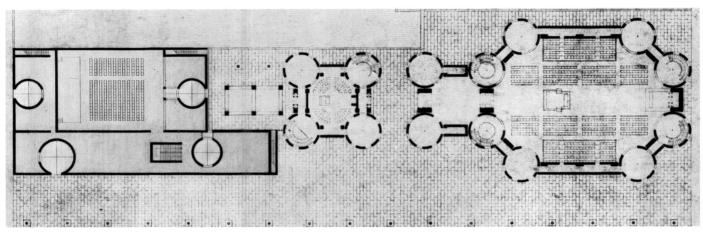

Window Rooms

Twenty feet in diameter and fifty-four feet high, each perimeter tower has glazed openings at the exterior and opposing, unglazed, arched openings to the interior—the ruins of Mikveh Israel (fig. 93). Whereas the Luanda ruins are simple planes, and the Salk ruins are exterior unglazed forms surrounding occupied space, the ruins of Mikveh are discrete inhabited interior cylinders of space. Fundamental to Kahn's design for Mikveh Israel is a main worship space with no openings to the exterior. This strategy forced Kahn, no doubt reluctantly, to incorporate glass into the exterior openings of the towers. Kahn struggled with a number of glazing alternatives, and arrived at a not entirely successful strategy of slicing across the cylinder, in one proposal, with a plane of leaded glass detached from exterior brick arches, which continue as exterior elements to complete the circle (fig. 95). In a third, more modernist proposal, an unglazed rectangular slot is cut into the cylinder and infilled with center-pivot wood windows (figs. 96, 97). In another proposal, the exterior opening is made up of a series of six smaller arched windows (fig. 98). Kahn continued to explore variations over the next several years (fig. 99). All of these strategies compromise the exterior reading of the ruin.

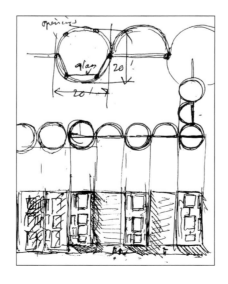

91 (top). Mikveh Israel Synagogue. First-floor plan, definitive state of sanctuary design. Dated October 29, 1963.

92 (above). Mikveh Israel Synagogue. Schematic model of early proposal.

93 (left). Mikveh Israel Synagogue. Study of "window room" configuration.

94 (opposite). Mikveh Israel Synagogue. View from tower looking toward sanctuary.

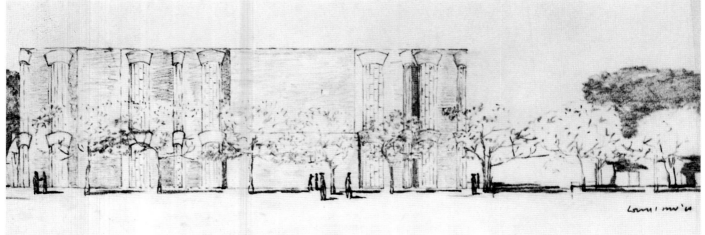

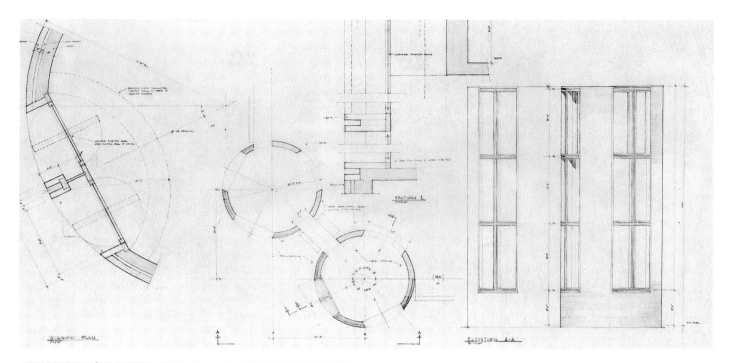

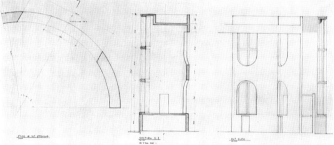

The openings to the interior, on the other hand, remain unglazed monumental arches in each of the design variations. All light entering the towers is filtered, softened, and diffused before entering the primary space. The sanctuary ceiling, a very shallow inverted dome, catches this diffused light (fig. 100)—an element of the design critical to the distribution of light in the interior, but an effect that Kahn never managed to represent in his interior perspectives (figs. 104, 105, 115). The result is ethereal, mysterious illumination. Kahn wrote in 1965:

The spaces are enclosed by window rooms 20 feet in diameter connected by walled passages. These window room elements have glazed openings on one exterior side and larger unglazed arched openings facing the interior. These rooms of light surrounding the synagogue chamber serve as an ambulatory and are high places for women. These window rooms prevail in the composition of the entrance chamber and the chapel across the way. In the community building, light is given to the interior by exterior roofless rooms born out of the same idea which, incidentally, gave rise to the plans at Dacca.

95 (opposite). Mikveh Israel Synagogue. Exterior perspective sketch showing leaded glass and brick arches at towers. Undated.

96 (top). Mikveh Israel Synagogue. Design studies of tower detailing: window plan, partial plan, section 1, elevation A-A. Inscribed 7 June 65.

97 (second from top). Mikveh Israel Synagogue. Design studies of tower detailing: section 2-2, interior elevation, c. June 1965.

98 (above). Mikveh Israel Synagogue. Exterior perspective sketch. Undated.

These windows on the outside do not support the building; what supports the building, as you can see on the plan, are the spaces between the windows. The windows could never be a support because of their shape. I chose to support the roof between the windows where a clear definition can be made between a column, a beam, and a wall. A column means a beam; a wall says a multitude of beams or a slab. They're different things.

In the model, the open spaces which make the window rooms independent of the structure are made too wide; but they are important to light the round shapes. The light from the exterior captured in the interior room of the window is seen from the synagogue chamber as free of glare. The whole idea comes from realizing that contrast of walls in the darkness against openings in light renders interior shapes illegible and turns the eyes away.[3]

It is a testament to the primal power of the image Kahn created that so much has been read into the cylinders of light that surround the sanctuary. Some see in these window-room towers of Mikveh Israel the medieval castles of Scotland, others the Aurelian walls in Rome, the columns of the Parthenon made hollow, the towers of Carcassonne, Brunelleschi's Santo Spirito, or the Tree of the Sephiroth.

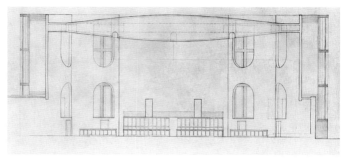

99 (top). Mikveh Israel Synagogue. Studies of exterior elevations. Inscribed Louis I. Kahn '64 and Redevelopment Authority, 27 April 1966.

100 (second from top). Mikveh Israel Synagogue. Longitudinal section through sanctuary. Undated, c. 1962.

101 (above). Mikveh Israel Synagogue. View toward ceiling of tower.

102 (opposite). Mikveh Israel Synagogue. View of diffused light entering sanctuary from towers.

103 (opposite). Mikveh Israel Synagogue. View from entry lobby toward sanctuary.

104 (top). Mikveh Israel Synagogue. Interior perspective of lobby with sanctuary beyond. Undated.

105 (right). Mikveh Israel Synagogue. Interior perspective of sanctuary. Undated.

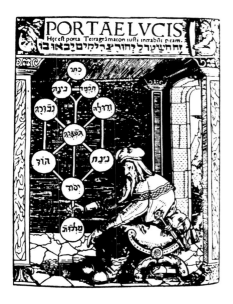

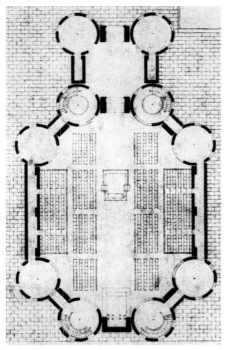

The Tree of the Sephiroth

The resemblance of Kahn's plan to the Kabbalistic image of the Tree of the Sephiroth is unmistakable. The Tree of the Sephiroth, or Tree of Life, is composed of ten circles, or major paths of wisdom, which increase in complexity and density. In the language of early Kabbalistic writers, the Sephiroth represented ten primeval aspects of God that propagated throughout the creation, like white light passing through a prism.[4] In another interpretation, one arrives at God by ascending the Tree of Life one Sephiroth at a time through meditation on the names of Jehovah.

Kahn's library included a book titled *Zohar,* with a cover illustration of a Jewish mystic contemplating the Sephiroth[5] (fig. 107). The center circle stands in for Kahn's bema, the lower circle for the entry space, the upper circle for the arc, and the surrounding circles for Kahn's light towers. Even the form of the diagram and the scale of the circles roughly correspond to Kahn's plan (fig. 108).

This direct connection, which Kahn never confirmed, is rendered suspect in light of the fact that the plan was developed by the fall of 1962 and *Zohar* was not published until 1963. In any event, Kahn's mother came from a long tradition of Jewish mysticism and was considered a "wise woman" in the Jewish community of Philadelphia where Kahn was raised. Her father, Abraham Mendelssohn (a relative of Felix Mendelssohn), was "a famous, well beloved Jewish mystic and spiritual healer in Riga."[6] It is quite likely that Kahn was long familiar with the Kabbalah and the Tree of the Sephiroth when he received the Mikveh commission. It is natural to read the cylinders of Mikveh as massive, hollow trunks of the Tree of Life providing a pathway to God. These towers, both physically and spiritually, are the single source of light for the congregation.

106 (opposite). Mikveh Israel Synagogue. View from ark toward bema.

107 (top). Tree of the Sephiroth. From Paulus Ricius, *Portae Lucis,* 1516.

108 (above). Mikveh Israel Synagogue. First-floor plan of sanctuary. Dated October 14, 1963.

109 (above left). Cathedral of Sainte Cecile, Albi, France. Pen and ink on paper. Inscribed Albi Lou K '59.

110 (above). Chapter house, Cathedral of Sainte Cecile, Albi, France. Pen and ink on paper. Inscribed Albi Lou K '59.

111 (opposite). Mikveh Israel Synagogue. View from bema toward ark.

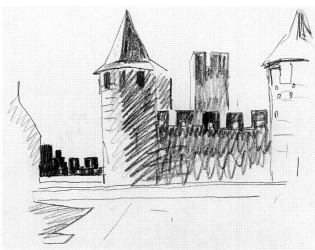

112 (opposite). Mikveh Israel Synagogue. View looking up toward arched opening of tower.

113 (top). City walls, Carcassonne, France. Pen and ink on paper, 1959. Inscribed Carcassonne.

114 (above). Fortifications, Carcassonne, France. Pencil on notebook paper, 1959. Inscribed Carcassonne.

Carcassonne

If Kahn's use of the Kabbalah is difficult to establish directly, there is physical evidence for other connections. In September 1959, Kahn attended the last meeting of the International Congress of Modern Architecture (CIAM), held in Otterlo. Before speaking at the congress, he traveled to France, where he made many sketches of the Cathedral of Sainte Cecile, Albi, and the medieval city of Carcassonne[7] (figs. 113, 114). Kahn's studies of the cathedral apse and the towers of the walled city show cylinders linking rectilinear forms, as at Mikveh (figs. 109, 110). These quick sketches—there are over thirty of them—seem to catalog with visual shorthand the elements Kahn found relevant in his search for formal archetypes—in sharp contrast to the studied watercolors of his 1929 travels, or the painterly saturated pastels of 1951. He referred to Carcassonne repeatedly for the remainder of his years. Speaking at the Otterlo conference he said:

We still want walls, we still want arches, arcades, and loggias of all kinds. We want all these things and, with that belief, need them. But they are not the character because a space today demands different things.[8]

Two years after his trip to France, in the midst of developing alternatives for Mikveh Israel, Kahn wrote:

A few years ago I visited Carcassonne. From the moment I entered the gates, I began to write with drawing, the images which I learned about, now presenting themselves to me like realized dreams. I began studiously to memorize in line the proportions and the living details of these great buildings. I spent the whole day in the courts, on the ramparts, and in the towers, diminishing my care about the proper proportions and exact details. At the close of the day I was inventing shapes and placing buildings in different relationships than they were.[9]

115 (opposite). Mikveh Israel
Synagogue. Perspective of
sanctuary. Pencil on notebook
paper, 1963.

116 (top). Mikveh Israel Synagogue.
View toward stair at tower.

117 (above). Mikveh Israel
Synagogue. View from tower
into sanctuary.

Castles

Another influence cannot be ignored: the castles of Scotland and England, which Kahn had sketched during his first visit to Europe (fig. 119). In March 1961—two months before beginning the design of Mikveh Israel—Kahn toured the castles of Scotland by air. He also had a number of books on castles that he referred to regularly. Reluctant to admit historical references, he nonetheless noted while working on Mikveh:

I have a book on castles and I try to pretend that I did not look at this book, but everybody reminds me of it, and I have to admit that I looked very thoroughly at this book.[10]

Ten years later Kahn discussed his interest in castles:

The Scottish Castle. Thick thick walls. Little openings to the enemy. Splayed inwardly to the occupant. A place to read, a place to sew . . . Places for the bed, for the stair . . . sunlight. Fairy Tale.[11]

At Carcassonne, as in the Scottish castles, the rectilinear walls that link taller cylindrical towers influenced the design of Mikveh Israel.

118 (left). Mikveh Israel Synagogue. View of sanctuary toward ark.

119 (above right). Caesar's Tower, Warwick Castle, England. Pencil on paper, 1928.

Ritual and the Architecture of Rome

Perhaps the most important connection between Mikveh Israel and the ancient world is not found in a specific borrowing of forms but rather in the influence of Frank E. Brown's ideas of Roman architecture and ritual. Mikveh Israel represents Kahn's first use of space as it was conceived by the ancient Romans—the configuration of discrete capsules to accommodate ritual:

The architecture of the Romans was, from first to last, an art of shaping space around ritual.[12]

With these words, Brown begins his beautiful book *Roman Architecture*, published just months before Kahn began work on Mikveh Israel. Kahn had arrived in Rome ten years earlier, just as Brown was refining his ideas about Roman ritual and space at the American Academy. Kahn often discussed these ideas with Brown as they visited Hadrian's Villa, the Flavian palace, Trajan's market, and Ostia.[13] Brown viewed early Romans as "congenitally disposed to be architects" even before they had developed the tools and materials to create monumental architecture. To Brown, the earliest Roman architects were priests who created elaborate rituals occupying rigidly defined capsules of space, even if this space was "invisible and impalpable." By the sixth century B.C.E., the Romans had thoroughly absorbed the art of building from the Greeks and Etruscans and began to give specific architectural expression to the rituals surrounding Roman religion, customs, traditions, discipline, and law:

Ritual is the art of action, but to the Romans it implied an art of another sort—architecture. The form of ritual is a fleeting form . . . but for the Romans it had the power to engender architectural form by the mere fact that it took place in space. Space was informed by ritual.[14]

120 (opposite). Mikveh Israel
Synagogue. View toward
exterior glazing at tower.

121 (above). Mikveh Israel
Synagogue. View from entrance to
women's gallery into sanctuary.

Roman architecture reached maturity in the second and third centuries C.E. with sophisticated forms to enclose the complex rituals of public worship, family life, public bathing, and assembly. Roman architects, according to Brown, created

huge cells of definite and concentrated function, walled off from the irrelevancy of other kinds of human activity . . . Roman architecture was an order of spaces shaped to constitute the environment of its moral order . . . The architects . . . sought spaces that would elevate, foster, prompt, and enforce but also describe the goals and their mutability, their dependence on the effort of individuals and collective attention and performance.[15]

From the time of his stay in Rome, Kahn insisted that architecture must reflect, contain, and reinforce the rituals and institutions of humanity. In many different ways, he expressed the idea that great architecture must begin with a questioning of the fundamental nature of the institution it is intended to serve. The words of Frank Brown almost echo in Kahn's discussions of architecture and the institutions of humanity. Kahn's famous distinction between Form and Design (which he capitalized to emphasize their importance) reflects this concern. To Kahn, Design was how an individual solves a particular problem, while Form had nothing to do with circumstantial acts. Form was arrived at through the discovery of an underlying, guiding, formal principle, linked to ritual and precedents. Kahn looked for the single big idea that could generate Form. The Phillips Exeter Academy library, for example, is based on the notion that a "man with a book goes to the light." This simple but almost metaphysical idea generates the form of the building "from first to last" by looking to the underlying relationship of humans to books and learning. It places books in relative darkness in the center of the building and draws readers to the exquisitely designed, naturally lit study carrels at the perimeter.

Kahn's work after his time in Rome increasingly took on the qualities of Roman space. Frank E. Brown describes the architecture of

122 (above). Mikveh Israel Synagogue. View of ark from bema.

123 (opposite). Mikveh Israel Synagogue. View of direct light entering towers.

124 (opposite). Mikveh Israel Synagogue. View from tower to tower diagonally across sanctuary.

125 (top). Mikveh Israel Synagogue. View from exterior into tower.

126 (above). Mikveh Israel Synagogue. View of direct light entering tower looking toward adjacent tower.

the Roman High Empire of 50 to 250 C.E., but his words could just as well describe the space and light of Kahn's work as it developed in the 1960s:

The spaces . . . were serenely bubblelike in volume and equilibrium. They were so proportioned as to clasp the activity they enveloped in a calmly finite encirclement . . . Light from high, in or under the vaults, articulated volume supplely by brilliance and sharp shadow or by the shimmer of reflection and veils of shade.[16]

House of Learning

As he began the design for Mikveh Israel, Kahn searched for the archetypal form of the synagogue—for the beginnings of religious ritual. Since the Jewish sanctuary is a *beis midrash,* or house of learning, he sought the essence of a place to teach and learn. The image of school and tree—whether or not the Tree of the Sephiroth—often figures prominently in Kahn's poetic musings:

Schools begin with a man under a tree who did not know he was a teacher discussing his realization with a few who did not know they were students . . . Soon spaces were erected and the first schools became. The establishment of School was inevitable because it was part of the desires of man . . . That is why it is good for the mind to go back to the beginning because the beginning of any established activity of man is its most wonderful moment. For in it lies all its spirit and resourcefulness from which we must constantly draw our inspirations of present needs. We can make our institutions great by giving them our sense of this inspiration in the architecture we offer them . . . School, the spirit school, the essence of the existence will, is what an architect must convey in his design.[17]

If there is any doubt that Kahn was, in part, thinking of ancient precedents, he continues his discussion of the school by saying:

In School as a realm of spaces where it is good to learn, the lobby . . . would become a generous Pantheon-like space where it is good to enter.[18]

One of Kahn's very early plans for Mikveh Israel incorporates a large circular lobby, which is arguably Kahn's Pantheon-like space (fig. 88). The diameter of the circle is almost half the length of the sanctuary it serves.

Kahn continued to work on Mikveh even after it became clear that the design committee of the congregation would not go forward. He continued to insist that the facility be separated into separate house of study, house of prayer, and house of community against the direction of the committee. Eventually Kahn was replaced, and a project developed by another architect was built. Mikveh Israel's abandonment was a case, all too common, of the vision of a great architect exceeding that of the client; of estimates surpassing budgets; of fundraising goals not realized; of Kahn's unwillingness to compromise core values—values that did not mesh entirely with those of the congregation. This uncompromising idealism, when reinforced by enlightened clients such as Jonas Salk or Richard Brown of the Kimbell Art Museum, made possible works of great subtlety, beautiful ambiguity, and depth. When Kahn worked with bureaucrats or committees, he was more often than not unsuccessful.

127 (opposite). Mikveh Israel Synagogue. View of stair at tower looking into sanctuary.

128 (left). Mikveh Israel Synagogue. View of direct light entering tower adjacent to entrance.

Memorial to
Six Million Jewish Martyrs

New York, New York, 1967–72

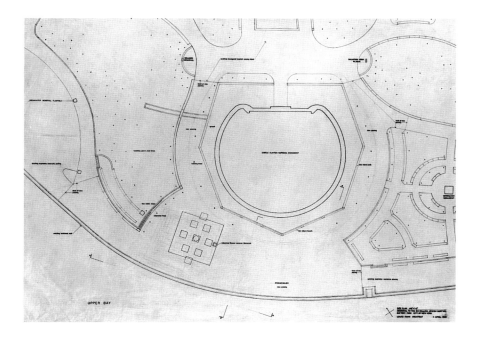

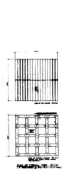

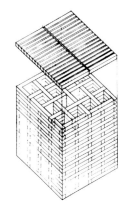

129 (preceding page). Memorial to Six Million Jewish Martyrs. View of seven-pier proposal from interior of central pier looking south.

130 (opposite). Memorial to Six Million Jewish Martyrs. View of seven-pier proposal looking toward New York Harbor.

131 (top). Memorial to Six Million Jewish Martyrs. Site plan showing Castle Clinton with seven-pier proposal. Dated 4 April 1968.

132 (above). Memorial to Six Million Jewish Martyrs. Isometric and glass-block layout of hollow pier. Dated October 25, 1967.

Efforts to create a Holocaust memorial in New York City span a period of fifty years. They began two years after the end of World War II with the designation by the city of a site for this purpose in Riverside Park.[1] They concluded in 1997 with the successful completion of Kevin Roche's Museum of Jewish Heritage, called "A Living Memorial to the Holocaust."

At least four designs were developed in the first twenty years after the war, including those of architect Eric Mendelsohn and sculptors Jo Davidson and Nathan Rapoport. Community concerns, an awkward decision-making process, and disagreement about literal versus abstract references to the horrors of the Holocaust kept all proposals from being adopted. In 1966, a subcommittee of the Committee for the Six Million, led by philanthropist David Lloyd Kreeger, was formed to revive the project. Architect Philip Johnson, a member of Kreeger's committee, recommended in 1967 that Kahn be given the commission.

A dramatic new site for the project had been chosen at the southernmost tip of Manhattan in Battery Park, with a view to New York Harbor, the Statue of Liberty, and Ellis Island. This was a fitting location for the monument, given the immigrant heritage of New York's large Jewish community. Directly adjacent to the site, the heavy stone fortress of Castle Clinton had been used to process immigrants prior to the completion of Ellis Island (fig. 131).

Kahn's initial solution for the memorial was simple and powerful: cast-glass piers sitting on a square, raised plinth. This use of glass is unique in Kahn's work, conceived at a time when he was developing sophisticated techniques for controlling light. Unlike the Kimbell Art Museum, the Phillips Exeter Academy library, or the Hurva Synagogue, where the major spaces are filled with complex interreflected luminous light falling on hard surfaces, the light of the memorial is refracted and transmitted. Images of water, sky, and distant monuments are transmitted and distorted. Rays of sunlight focus and spread as they pass through multiple layers of thick transparent glass. Kahn initially conceived of the piers as cast into huge single blocks of glass, but a visit to the Corning glassworks made it apparent that this was not technically feasible. Kahn settled on a strategy of cast bricks of glass six inches by six inches, in lengths that varied from eighteen inches to eight feet (fig. 132):

The piers are constructed with solid blocks of glass placed one over the other and interlocking without the use of mortar, reminiscent of how the Greeks laid their solid blocks in their temples. The top of each pier is sealed with thin layers of lead set into specially molded joints. The entire construction in depth will be evident as one looks through each pier and through the entire composition of piers.[2]

All of Kahn's studies for this monument are perfectly square in plan. The square plan can be found in many of Kahn's projects, particularly when the architecture was conceived to express what Kahn considered powerful fundamentals. Five nested squares were used at the Trenton bathhouse, of which Kahn said "I discovered myself" in his search for an architectural vision (see fig. 24). The plan of the Exeter library, under design when Kahn began work on the memorial, is square (see fig. 164). At Exeter, Kahn looked to express the very origins of knowledge and learning. The square was used for the first proposals for the Mikveh Israel Synagogue, where Kahn began his search for the origins of Jewish ritual (see fig. 86), and in the Hurva Synagogue, where he attempted to develop a new monument for all of Judaism adjacent to the Western Wall of King Solomon's Temple (see figs. 162, 163).

The first study for the memorial placed four groupings of three tall, narrow glass piers around one large center monolith. This produced a total of thirteen glass structures—perhaps an unfortunate number given the interest in numerology of some of those on the Committee for the Six Million (fig. 133). The studies that followed over the next several months featured nine glass piers, all of the same dimension—eight at the perimeter

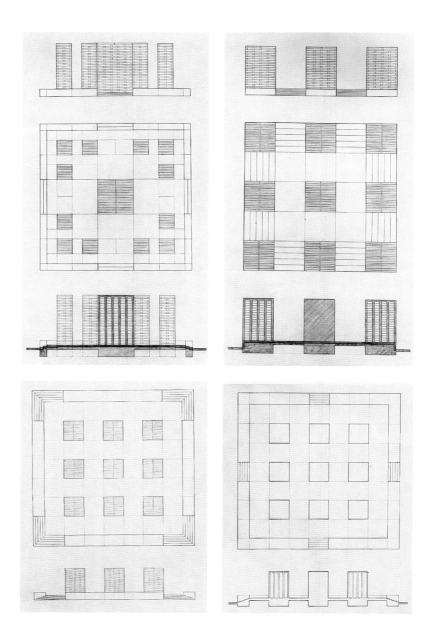

133 (top left). Memorial to Six Million Jewish Martyrs. Elevation, plan, and section, thirteen-pier proposal, 1967.

134 (top right). Memorial to Six Million Jewish Martyrs. Elevation, plan, and section, first nine-pier proposal with steps between piers, 1967.

135 (above left). Memorial to Six Million Jewish Martyrs. Plan and section, nine-pier proposal on base with corner steps, 1967.

136 (above right). Memorial to Six Million Jewish Martyrs. Plan and section, nine-pier proposal on base with corner benches, 1967.

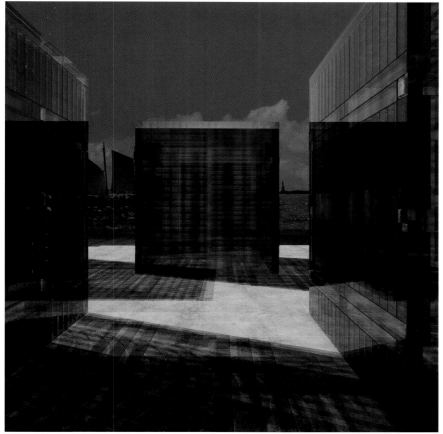

137 (top). Memorial to Six Million Jewish Martyrs.
Perspective view of nine-pier proposal from Castle
Clinton, 1967.

138 (above). Memorial to Six Million Jewish Martyrs.
View of seven-pier proposal looking toward New
York Harbor.

139 (overleaf). Memorial to Six Million Jewish
Martyrs. View of nine-pier proposal with corner
benches looking toward Castle Clinton.

and one in the center (fig. 134). Kahn explored several variations in the design of the plinth during the next few months: a corner step arrangement with central benches (fig. 135), and a central step arrangement with corner benches (figs. 136, 137).

The proposal first presented to the Kreeger committee in November 1967 consists of a five-by-five grid, with three rows of three identical glass piers set to the edge of an upper platform. Steps lead to each of the eight voids from a lower plinth. Although the design provides perfect biaxial symmetry, there is no circulation at either central axis, as might be expected; the center is occupied by solids of glass. The dimension of each void equals that of each solid and creates the rhythm of light-shadow-light-shadow of which Kahn so often spoke.

Kahn resisted pressure to create a more literal representation of the Holocaust and chose instead to try to convey idealism, hope, and triumph. Such ideas could find expression only in abstraction. Writing in the third person, Kahn discussed his choice of glass:

The Architect's central thought was that the Monument should present a non accusing character, and he thought of glass for its quality of material presence yet the sun could come through and leave a shadow yet filled with light. Not like marble or stone with its defined shadow; the stone could be accusing, the glass could not . . .

The site, in wake of its signs of "Welcome to America"—Ellis Island, Castle Garden, the Statue of Liberty—did much to inspire the use of glass, the sense of dematerialization to allow all of these symbolic structures, and all life around, to enter the Monument.[3]

He also wrote:

Changes of light, the seasons of the year, the play of weather, and the drama of movement on the river will transmit their life to the monument.[4]

Symbolism forced Kahn to compromise this first proposal. The Committee for the Six Million included several Talmudic scholars who pointed out that in Jewish numerology the number nine is equated with human gestation, childbirth, and the bringing of life into the world; it was thus an inappropriate symbol for a monument commemorating those who died at Nazi hands in the Holocaust. Some committee members suggested that the number six be incorporated to refer to the six million martyrs. Others remained uncomfortable with the lack of recognizable figurative elements in the design.[5]

Kahn accepted this criticism and quickly reworked the proposal. The Kreeger committee unanimously approved a revised design of six perimeter piers and a central unique pier, but the Committee for the Six Million rejected it after a heated and emotional meeting in late 1967. Many members were still concerned that Kahn's proposal was too abstract. A letter to Kahn written one week after the rejection explained the reaction of those who had directly experienced the Holocaust:

As you undoubtedly noted from the reaction of those who suffered the most, not all present felt that your model totally fulfilled their longings, represented their thoughts, or relieved their tragic memories.[6]

140 (opposite). Memorial to Six Million Jewish Martyrs. Perspective view of seven-pier proposal with central shrine. Inscribed LIK 3 Dec '67 1968.

141 (above). Memorial to Six Million Jewish Martyrs. View of seven-pier proposal with central shrine.

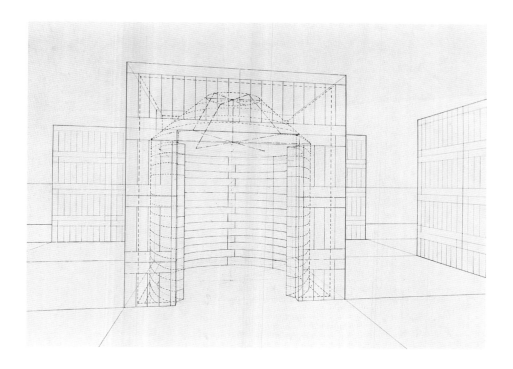

142 (above left). Memorial to Six Million Jewish Martyrs. View of seven-pier proposal from interior of central shrine looking toward New York Harbor.

143 (above). Memorial to Six Million Jewish Martyrs. View of seven-pier proposal from interior of central shrine looking north.

144 (left). Memorial to Six Million Jewish Martyrs. Perspective view of seven-pier proposal looking toward central shrine, 1967.

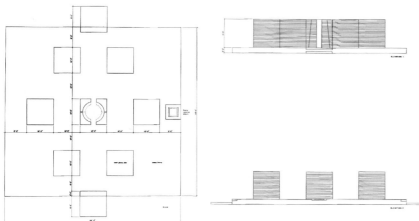

145 (top). Memorial to Six Million Jewish Martyrs. Model of seven-pier proposal built for the exhibition "Louis I. Kahn: In the Realm of Architecture," 1992–94.

146 (above). Memorial to Six Million Jewish Martyrs. Elevations and plan, seven-pier proposal with central shrine. Dated 4 April 1968.

147 (left). Memorial to Six Million Jewish Martyrs. View of seven-pier proposal looking toward New York Harbor.

Three weeks after the rejection, Kahn and six members of the Committee for the Six Million signed an agreement that stipulated that the central pier would be developed into a shrine of the same material as the six pillars, but with some lilac in its color. The walls of the shrine were to have several suitable inscriptions in Yiddish, Hebrew, and English, both on the outside and the inside. The ceiling of the shrine would bear some artistic Jewish symbol.[7]

Kahn introduced these more literal elements in a series of alternate proposals that followed. This culminated in a design, presented with a large model, of a single low plinth accessed on two sides by two risers (figs. 140, 144, 146). It may be coincidental that the plan of this proposal again resembles the Tree of the Sephiroth (see fig. 107). The central pier was hollow, with an opening on the south side to New York Harbor. It contained a cylindrical chapel with inscriptions etched into the glass bricks. Kahn said of this revised proposal:

The Architect reflected on the prevailing desire to give the Monument a sense of the ritualistic, causing him to change the nine piers to seven, in which the center pier is given the character of a little chapel, open to the sky, into which a small group or family could enter. The chapel interior and the outside of this pier is to be inscribed. The six piers around the center, of equal dimensions, are not inscribed. The one then, the chapel, speaks; the other six are silent . . . The six and one stand on a granite base, 66 feet by 66 feet square, high enough to sit on its edge. Each glass pier is 10 feet by 10 feet square and 11 feet high. The space separating each pier is equal to the dimension of the pier itself.[8]

This proposal was accepted, and the New York City Art Commission granted its preliminary approval to Kahn's design in April 1968. But with a final design at long last in hand after a difficult design process, the project collapsed due to inadequate funds, and Kahn's fee, billed in June, went unpaid.

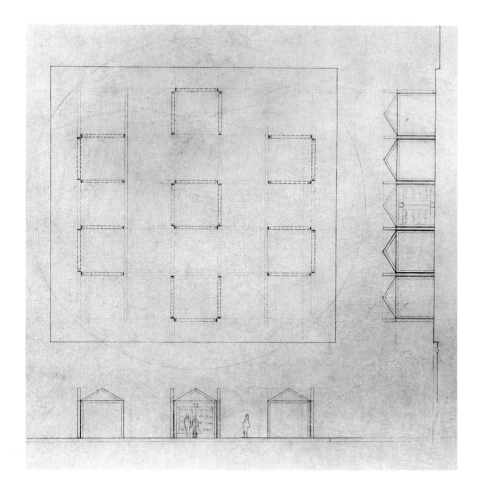

There was a brief revival of efforts to build the monument. The Committee for the Six Million at last paid Kahn's fee and invited him to revise the design using conventional materials with no glass. The basic parti was kept, but gabled structures were substituted for the glass piers (fig. 149). The effort seems half-hearted—perhaps it is just as well that this pale reflection of Kahn's original vision was never built.

148 (opposite). Memorial to Six Million Jewish Martyrs. View of seven-pier proposal looking north.

149 (above). Memorial to Six Million Jewish Martyrs. Section, plan, and elevation, final proposal, 1972.

Hurva Synagogue, First Proposal

Jerusalem, Israel, 1967–68

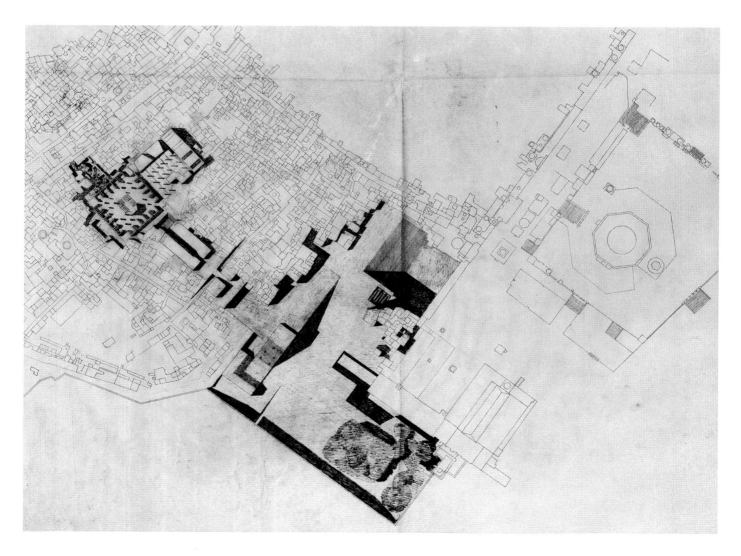

Kahn incorporated elements of the ruin into most of his architecture after the design of the U.S. Consulate in Luanda. In 1967 he received a commission to replace a destroyed synagogue in Jerusalem called Hurva, which translates from the Hebrew—through a marvelous coincidence—as "ruin."

At the beginning of the eighteenth century, Jerusalem's first Ashkenazi synagogue was built with money borrowed from Arab lenders. When the borrowers defaulted in 1721, the lenders demolished the building, thus leading to the name Hurva.[1] In the nineteenth century, a second synagogue was constructed on the site. This rather heavy-handed structure resembled a Turkish mosque, just as most Jewish architecture has tended to adopt the prevailing style of the local majority religion. The new Hurva synagogue was the largest in the Old City, used for installation of the chief rabbis. It dominated the quarter's skyline on the hill west of the Dome of the Rock. This Hurva was once again destroyed, along with fifty-seven other Jewish religious structures, by the Jordanian army as the Old City was secured during the war of 1948.

Soon after the Jewish quarter came under Israeli control in 1967, discussions began regarding the ruined remains of the old Hurva. The architect Ram Karmi was approached to build a new Hurva by the owners of the site. Karmi declined the commission, saying that a new synagogue for a new state was needed—and that only Louis I. Kahn should undertake such an important and challenging project. Karmi's sister Ada, along with patron Yaacov Salomon, traveled to Philadelphia to convince Kahn to accept the commission, which Kahn did without hesitation. Jerusalem mayor Teddy Kollek became, in effect, Kahn's client and one of his main proponents in the project.

For Kahn, this project presented an extraordinary opportunity to express his most deeply felt ideas about architecture. This was his chance to build the great Jewish monument at the religious center of the new Jewish state—in the very region where

150 (preceding page). Hurva Synagogue, first proposal. View from concrete tower into sanctuary.

151 (opposite top). Hurva Synagogue, first proposal. Section through site showing Hurva at left and the Dome of the Rock at right, 1968.

152 (opposite bottom). Hurva Synagogue, first proposal. Site plan of old quarter, 1968.

153 (above right). Ruins of the previous Hurva Synagogue, destroyed 1947.

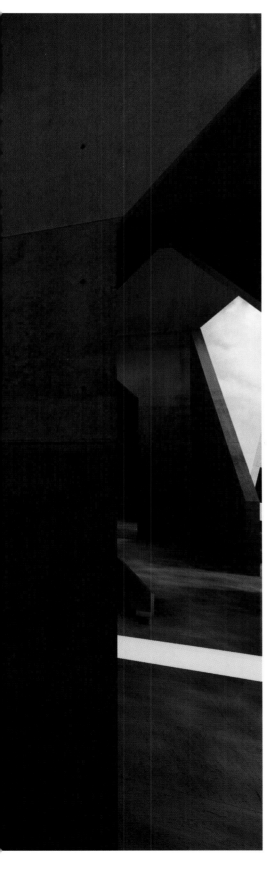

154. Hurva Synagogue, first proposal. View from pylon on second level toward sanctuary.

the three major Western religions were born. As the world's leading Jewish architect, Kahn was conscious of the huge responsibility of this commission. In addition, Hurva was Kahn's first and only opportunity to build in the context of ancient ruins (figs. 152, 153). Fascinated by the tradition of "assembly," he saw the synagogue as a rare opportunity to create a place where people could gather to transcend individual concerns.

Kahn conceived of the new Hurva as the third great religious monument of Jerusalem, to take its place with the Muslim Dome of the Rock and the Christian Church of the Holy Sepulcher. He was clearly inspired by the location, and a beautiful pencil drawing of the site places the new Hurva confidently on the skyline of Jerusalem, balancing the prominence of the Dome of the Rock (fig. 151). Kahn used to tell his students that great architecture was the result of a very lonely and difficult search for personal expression and inspiration. Shortly after presenting his first design for Hurva, Kahn wrote to the Ministerial Committee for Jerusalem:

I received your letter with joy to know that I have been honored to express the spirit of history and religion of Jerusalem through my design [of the Hurva] and its environs . . . The idea which motivated the design I submitted for your approval some months ago came from inspirations never before felt.[2]

Precedents
As he had done with Mikveh Israel, Kahn began the design of Hurva with a search for the very beginnings of Jewish religious form and ritual. He requested an article written in 1930 by Louis Finkelstein called "The Origin of the Synagogue" from the librarian of the Jewish Theological Seminary in New York, no doubt expecting that a work of that title would be helpful in this quest.[3] Finkelstein does refer to King Solomon's Temple as the true archetype of Jewish architecture, but the article included neither drawings nor photographs and was filled with arcane references to religious texts. Kahn, who

155 (above). Hurva Synagogue, first proposal. Study of ambient light on second level, tower-to-tower view.

156 (opposite). Hurva Synagogue, first proposal. Study of ambient light on second level, tower-to-tower view.

157 (overleaf). Hurva Synagogue, first proposal. View from pylon on second level toward zone between inner and outer building.

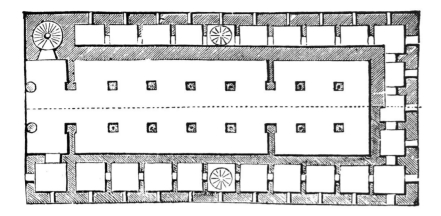

158 (opposite). Hurva Synagogue, first proposal. View from tower at second level toward gap between pylons.

159 (top). Temple of Solomon, Jerusalem, Israel, 1015 B.C.E. Conjectural plan. From *History of Architecture* by James Fergusson.

160 (above). Hurva Synagogue, first proposal. Study of ambient light on second level, view from stair into ambulatory at pylons.

161 (overleaf). Hurva Synagogue, first proposal. View from ambulatory at second level of pylons.

devoured visual information and claimed to be "a rather interesting kind of scholar because I don't read and I don't write,"[4] probably found it to be of little use other than to encourage an investigation of Solomon's Temple—whose Western Wall was only a short walk from the Hurva site. Another publication in Kahn's library was James Fergusson's *History of Architecture*, which included a highly speculative reconstruction of the temple (fig. 159). The square plan of the most sacred inner chamber of this reconstruction would have been of interest to Kahn.

But the Fergusson plan showed more than just a square chamber. Four massive columns defined the square central space, and an ambulatory ran around the perimeter through a series of smaller rooms. Kahn had deployed this very parti in the design of the Phillips Exeter Academy library, where he tried to express the beginnings of learning and knowledge (fig. 164). The Exeter library is a building within a building: the inner space is lit from above and built from concrete, while the outer building is of brick. Between the outer and inner structures is a complex ambulatory that permits circumnavigation of the building. The Hurva plan is similar, as Kahn explained:

The new building should itself consist of two buildings—an outer one which would absorb the light and heat of the sun, and an inner one, giving the effect of a separate but related building . . . the exterior will be visible through the niches which are in the stones.[5]

The outer building of Hurva consists of sixteen massive pylons of load-bearing Jerusalem stone, four to a side, recalling some ancient monumental ruin, perhaps from Egypt, or even from some more remote past now lost to history (fig. 167). The pylon forms of Hurva were foreshadowed in Kahn's 1951 pastel drawings of the Ptolemaic Temple at Edfu, the Temple of Amon at Luxor, and the Temple of Amon at Karnak (figs. 170–72, 180). Although the plan shows perfect biaxial symmetry, Hurva can be entered only at the four open corners

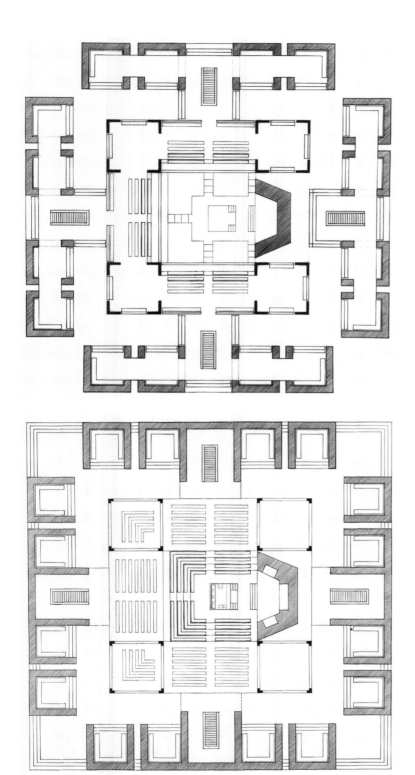

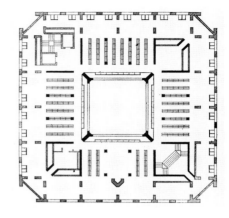

162 (top left). Hurva Synagogue, first proposal. Mezzanine plan, c. July 1968.

163 (left). Hurva Synagogue, first proposal. First-floor plan, c. July 1968.

164 (top). Library, Phillips Exeter Academy, Exeter, New Hampshire, 1965–72. Fourth-floor plan.

165 (above). Hurva Synagogue, first proposal. View from tower at second level toward gap between pylons.

166 (opposite top). Hurva Synagogue, first proposal. Section sketch. Dated 15 July 1968.

167 (opposite middle). Hurva Synagogue, first proposal. Scale model, 1968.

168 (opposite bottom). Hurva Synagogue, first proposal. Section-perspective.

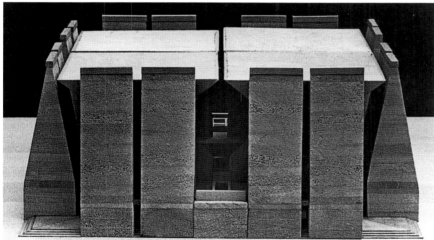

through narrow gaps between the pylons, rather than on axis as might be expected in a Beaux-Arts plan of similar symmetry (fig. 163).

On the main level, the pylons are carved out to create, in essence, small chapels lit at night by candles:

There are niches where candle services will be sung during certain ceremonies . . . I sensed the light of a candle plays an important part in Judaism . . . I felt this was an extension of the source of religion as well as an extension of the practice of Judaism.[6]

At the upper level, an ambulatory passes through openings in the pylon sides (fig. 162). This is strikingly similar to the ambulatory of Fergusson's reconstruction, where narrow side openings lead from square niche to square niche.

At the Luanda consulate, the enclosing "ruin walls" were to be of a very modern cast concrete, while the inner building was constructed from blocks of limestone—resulting in an unclear reading of "old" and "new." At Exeter, the outer ruins are of brick, like Roman ruins, while the inner building is concrete—a much clearer reading. At Hurva, Kahn selected the Jerusalem stone of the ancient structures in the area for the enclosing pylons, while employing concrete, as at Exeter, for the inner sanctuary. This contrast of material creates Kahn's most literal expression of "ruins wrapped around buildings":

These stones are 16 feet square, the interior chambers are 10 foot square. The stones, like the stones of the Western Wall, will be golden in color; the interior will be rather silver in color . . . I intend to use the same stone as the stones of the Western Wall, large, not small stones, rather as large as you can get, as monolithic looking as possible . . . With concrete it is very beautiful. If it is beautifully done, it is one of the finest of materials.[7]

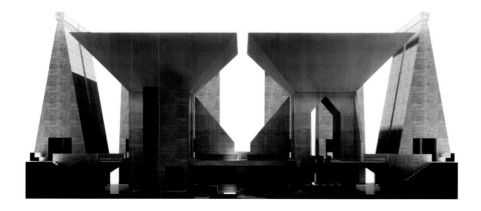

169 (opposite). Hurva Synagogue, first proposal. View of pylon looking toward Jerusalem.

170 (top). Ptolemaic Temple, Edfu, Egypt. Study of pylon. Pastel on paper, 1951.

171 (second from top). Hypostyle Hall and Pylon of Ramses II, Temple of Amon, Luxor, Egypt. Pastel on paper. Inscribed Louis I. Kahn '51.

172 (above). Southeast pylons, Temple of Amon, Karnak, Egypt. Pastel on paper. Inscribed Lou K '51.

Hurva's Inner Chamber

Hurva's inner chamber is a sanctuary of concrete and shadows, protected and enclosed by the primitive pylon forms. At both Exeter and Hurva, four hollow concrete columns occupy the corners of the inner structure (containing stairs and rest rooms at Exeter, and seating and circulation to the balconies at Hurva). The openings cut into the thin concrete planes of Hurva seem, like the pylons, to reveal vague historical references—perhaps Egyptian or even an angular Gothic. Their placement results in a complex layering of elements.

The bema, or altar from which the Torah is read, is placed precisely in the center of the sanctuary, surrounded by seating for an intimate daily service of two hundred. The bema faces the ark carved into a U-shaped wall, several feet thick, built of the same stone as the pylons. On each axis are located steps to the second floor, which lead to the pylon ambulatory and to three separate balcony sections linked through openings in the hollow concrete columns. During the larger services, the space between towers and pylons becomes a *beis knesset*, or house of assembly, where the crowds of the High Holy Days can gather comfortably.

Kahn's section reveals the complexity of Hurva's design, with a fascinating space created at the juncture of inner and outer, where the four sloping sections of the massive concrete ceiling do not quite touch the opposing pylons (figs. 166, 174):

The spaces between them will be such as to allow a sufficient amount of light to enter the outer chamber, and completely surrounding the interior chamber . . . the construction of the building is like large leaves of a tree, allowing light to filter into the interior.[8]

As he did with Mikveh Israel, Kahn makes a tree analogy for this *beis midrash*, or house of learning, where learning first began "under a tree." The section shows the ceiling elements almost touching at a central crossing, while the model developed later shows a two-foot gap at their intersection,

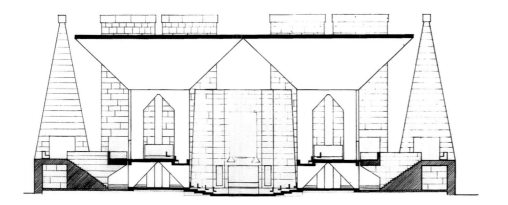

173 (above). Hurva Synagogue, first proposal. View at transition from inner sanctuary to outer building.

174 (left). Hurva Synagogue, first proposal. Section. Pencil on vellum, 1968.

175 (opposite). Hurva Synagogue, first proposal. View from tower to tower.

176 (above). Hurva Synagogue, first proposal. Study of direct light entering inner sanctuary.

177 (opposite). Hurva Synagogue, first proposal. Study of ambient light entering inner sanctuary.

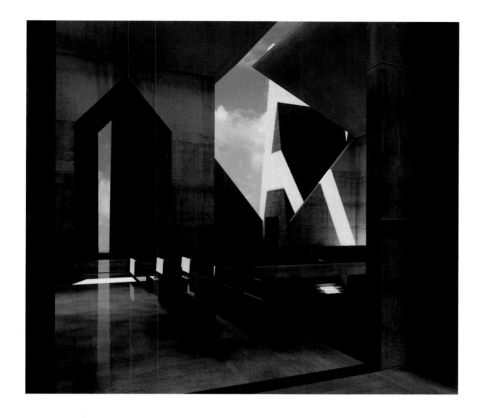

178 (opposite). Hurva Synagogue, first proposal. View from pylon on second level toward inner sanctuary.

179 (top). Hurva Synagogue, first proposal. View from tower at second level toward inner sanctuary.

180 (above). Hypostyle Hall, Temple of Amon, Karnak, Egypt. Inscribed Louis I. Kahn '51.

181 (overleaf). Hurva Synagogue, first proposal. View from ark on first level.

the source of the complex light that enters the interior. Kahn wrote:

The outside of the building belongs to the sun, the interior belongs to the shadows. It is a place where people live.[9]

The Hurva Synagogue could have been one of the great experiments with the manipulation of sunlight. Few architects have ever created space with such presence, and this was certainly one of Kahn's strongest ideas. At Hurva, Kahn had an opportunity to work with the intense light of the desert, rendered so powerfully in his travel sketches of Egypt fifteen years earlier. By separating the ceiling forms with a cross-shaped opening to the sky and leaving gaps between the heavy pylons, a marvelous pattern of shafts of sunlight strikes the interior.

But Kahn's use of light in Hurva went well beyond just patterns of sunlight, only the most obvious feature. He created a zone between pylons and sanctuary as a light-diffusing and light-coloring device—a logical extension of techniques previously developed for the Salk meeting house, the Luanda consulate, and the Mikveh Israel Synagogue. When intense sunlight strikes the upper pylons, a diffused yellow light is thrown onto the adjacent ceiling. The concrete, in turn, reflects an even softer luminous light back onto the lower portion of the pylons. This intermediate zone between interior and exterior—a fascinating space where the tapering pylons and sloping ceiling planes never quite touch—creates constantly changing lighting effects, magical and luminous. The pylons are both the sun walls and the ruins of Hurva. The light of Hurva is the light of the Pantheon.

World Synagogue

The design for a new Hurva stimulated much interest and controversy in Israel. It was discussed in the Knesset and displayed at the Israel Museum, and it was the object of much coverage in the press. Kahn's correspondence with those in Israel indicate the depth of support for his proposal. Many there shared Kahn's vision. Teddy Kollek

called it the "world synagogue." Yaacov Salomon praised the solution, and Kahn replied:

I am grateful for your letter telling me of the favorable reception my work received. The conception presented was a development of what I realized from the very beginning to be the Form and its elements . . . the design had the essence of Hurva's spirit and the desire to be.[10]

Ten days later, Jerusalem mayor Teddy Kollek wrote to Kahn:

It has been a long time since a single subject such as your plans for the Hurva has aroused as wide a response, and this, of course, not only in Jerusalem but throughout the country. The decision concerning your plans is essentially a political one. Should we in the Jewish quarter have a building of major importance which "competes" with the Mosque and the Holy Sepulcher, and should we in general have any building which would compete in importance with the Western Wall of the Temple.[11]

After the presentation of the first proposal for Hurva, Kahn did little work on the synagogue for the next year.

182 (opposite). Hurva Synagogue, first proposal. View from bema up to ceiling.

183 (top). Hurva Synagogue, first proposal. View of zone between inner and outer structures at second level behind ark.

184 (above). Hurva Synagogue, first proposal. View from under balcony toward inner sanctuary.

185 (opposite). Hurva Synagogue, first proposal. View from pylon on second level toward tower.

186 (top). Hurva Synagogue, first proposal. View of ambulatory at pylons on second level.

187 (above right). Hurva Synagogue, first proposal. Study of light at stair from lower level to second level.

188 (above far right). Hurva Synagogue, first proposal. Study of light at stair from lower level to second level.

189 (above). Hurva Synagogue, first proposal. View from pylon on second level toward inner sanctuary.

190 (opposite top). Hurva Synagogue, first proposal. View from pylon on second level toward inner sanctuary.

191 (opposite bottom). Hurva Synagogue, first proposal. View from pylon on second level toward tower.

192 (opposite). Hurva Synagogue, first proposal. View from pylon on lower level toward tower.

193 (top). Hurva Synagogue, first proposal. View from pylon on lower level toward tower.

194 (above right). Hurva Synagogue, first proposal. View from pylon on lower level toward tower.

195 (far right). Hurva Synagogue, first proposal. View from tower at lower level toward pylons.

Hurva Synagogue, Second Proposal

Jerusalem, Israel, 1969

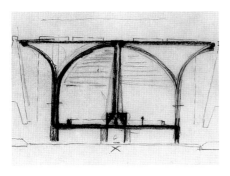

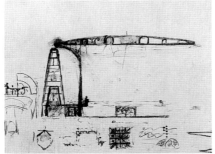

In June and July 1969, Kahn briefly resumed work on the design of the Hurva Synagogue. Studies in his notebooks reveal that he considered various arrangements for the inner sanctuary, including domes and vaults (figs. 197, 199). He soon settled on a radical new proposal: a massive shell, square in plan, that curved outward from the balcony level (figs. 200, 203, 204). Light penetrated this shell only at narrow slots cut into the center of each of the four shell segments and at a six-inch gap between the shell's top and the flat ceiling. No light entered from above. It created a dark, brooding, mysterious interior. Kahn described the project in a talk:

This chamber should be more anonymous, I feel more deeply, not knowing in what direction it should go. And therefore, you might say that it sums up, you see, a new beginning of a chamber which, by practice, will become a ritual as the State of Israel today—with the various attitudes that are about religion can take place. So therefore, even the Torah, the Ark, is not present in these chambers as I see it now, but is in one of these niches . . . where it can be taken out, as it used to be done when there was a procession . . . So the Ark is there . . . or you might say the synagogue is the Ark . . . a very precious building.[1]

An Architecture out of Scale

In this new Hurva, all elements referring to human scale were eliminated. Without doors, without seating, without views, without detail, and without recognizable religious objects, Kahn purposely attempted to create a presence linked to divinity rather than to human scale. Gone was the complex layering of spaces and views across and through the sanctuary found in the first proposal. The ark, tucked away behind columns and under the balcony, is no longer the prominent element (fig. 207). The upper ambulatory through the pylons, with its series of intimately scaled chambers, is omitted (fig. 206). The shell, cantilevered at the corners, seems to balance precariously on four paired columns adjacent to the center stairs. This strange curved shell of the sanctuary, which grows ever wider as it reaches great height, is difficult to relate to any other known form.

196 (preceding page). Hurva Synagogue, second proposal. View of zone between inner and outer structures.

197 (opposite). Hurva Synagogue, second proposal. Study sketches, 1969.

198 (top). Hurva Synagogue, second proposal. View of shell of sanctuary from between pylons.

199 (above left). Hurva Synagogue, second proposal. Study section of vaulted interior chamber, 1969.

200 (above right). Hurva Synagogue, second proposal. Study section of curved outer shell. Dated 19 June 1969.

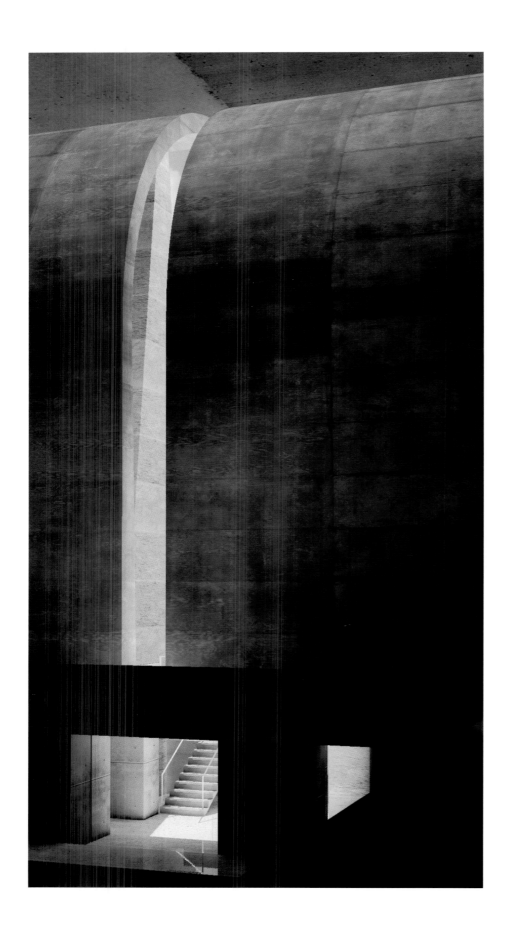

201 (left). Hurva Synagogue, second proposal. View of slot at sanctuary shell from balcony.

202 (opposite top). Hurva Synagogue, second proposal. View of slot at sanctuary shell from balcony.

203 (opposite bottom left). Hurva Synagogue, second proposal. Sketch of section of curved outer shell, 1969.

204 (opposite bottom right). Hurva Synagogue, second proposal. Drafted section of curved outer shell, 1969.

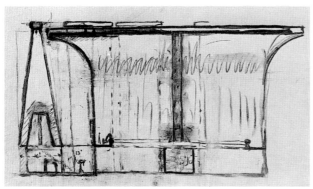

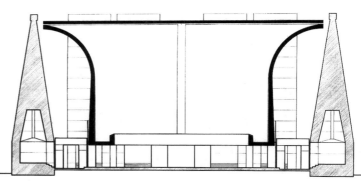

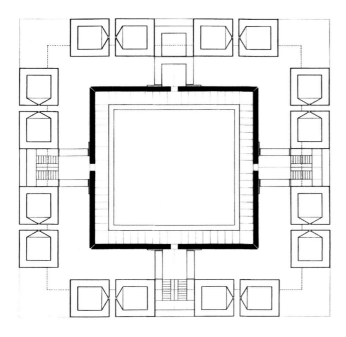

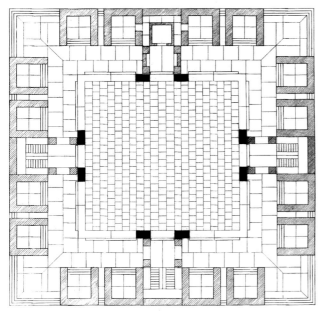

205 (opposite). Hurva Synagogue, second proposal. View of slot at sanctuary shell from stair.

206 (top). Hurva Synagogue, second proposal. Mezzanine plan, 1969.

207 (above). Hurva Synagogue, second proposal. First-floor plan, 1969.

The second proposal for Hurva demonstrates a trend that can be found in much of Kahn's later work: a turning away from the transparent and hygienic space championed by Le Corbusier in the 1920s and 1930s in favor of the architecture of the sublime as expressed by Etienne-Louis Boullée, Claude-Nicolas Ledoux, and such philosophers as Burke and Kant in the late eighteenth century. In his poem "Twelve Lines," Kahn wrote:

Spirit in the will to express
can make the great sun seem small.
the sun is
Thus the universe.
Did we need Bach
Bach is
Thus music is
Did we need Boullée
Did we need Ledoux
Boullée is
Ledoux is
Thus Architecture is.[2]

Kahn's design for Hurva expresses a fascination with shadows, veils, and mystery—a space, as Foucault writes, of "darkened spaces, of pall and gloom which prevents the full visibility of things, men and truths."[3] Kahn came closer than any other architect of the twentieth century to creating an architecture of the sublime. In his essay "Form and Design," Kahn wrote:

Even a space intended to be dark should have just
enough light from some mysterious opening to tell us
how dark it really is . . . A great building, in my
opinion, must begin with the unmeasurable, must
go through the measurable means when it is being
designed and in the end must be unmeasurable . . .
what is unmeasurable is the psychic spirit.[4]

Kahn's second design for Hurva was raw and primal—even threatening. He sought to induce the sort of pleasurable threat that comes from standing on the edge of a cliff—a tranquillity tinged with terror. Kahn felt that it was a crime to purposely make something beautiful. He hated the precious, the contrived, the decorative. As Burke wrote:

208 (opposite). Hurva Synagogue, second proposal. View toward curved shell of sanctuary.

209 (top left). Hurva Synagogue, second proposal. View toward curved shell of sanctuary.

210 (top right). Hurva Synagogue, second proposal. View toward curved shell of sanctuary.

211 (above left). Hurva Synagogue, second proposal. View toward curved shell of sanctuary.

212 (above right). Hurva Synagogue, second proposal. View toward curved shell of sanctuary.

213 (overleaf). Hurva Synagogue, second proposal. View from stair at lower level into sanctuary.

Sublime objects are vast in their dimensions, beautiful ones comparatively small; beauty should be smooth and polished; the great rugged and negligent . . . beauty should be light and delicate; the great ought to be solid, and even massive.[5]

Ambiguous Materials

By the early 1960s, Kahn had developed a vocabulary of materials to which he returned over and over during the last years of his life—ambiguous materials with rich associations and long histories, both old and new at the same time. He continually referred to the light and form of the Pantheon in Rome as a source of inspiration. Although he did not emphasize the materials of the Pantheon, it is likely that this aspect also influenced his thinking. The interior wall surfaces of the Pantheon are surprisingly intact after so many years, yet darkened with age and soot and scarred by thousands of minor and major mishaps. The gray concrete dome—perhaps the very first ambitious use of concrete in architecture— soaks up light like a sponge. The walls, floor, and dome have the beautiful patina of the ancient. The effect is quite different from Hadrian's day, when the marble facings must have been polished and brilliantly reflective. Light falling on those clean smooth surfaces was bright and clear. This is the light found in the white plaster churches of Aalto and Palladio. Many, no doubt Kahn included, would prefer the effects of the Pantheon as it has aged. At Hurva and elsewhere, Kahn's concrete has this patina of the ancient.

Kahn used concrete for both structure and finish in almost all of his major interior spaces after 1959. For Kahn, and for Le Corbusier as well, concrete had the ability to spring immediately from its formwork pre-aged, marked by the pour, streaked with water stains, and suffering the spalls and trauma of the construction process. Kahn's concrete, more so than Le Corbusier's, was a fine and beautiful cast stone, with depth and subtle finish. Kahn and his associates went to great lengths to develop the exact mix of formwork, admixtures, and sand to achieve the perfect color, depth, and texture. Like the aged surfaces of the

Pantheon, Kahn's concrete absorbs as much light as it reflects—like sooty ancient stone—creating beautiful chiaroscuro effects. This result is particularly noticeable in dark spaces such as the second Hurva, where slashes of light entering through the slits scatter to create the softest possible illumination.

Travertine, the stone of the Romans, can also be found in almost all of Kahn's later projects: the plaza of the Salk Institute laboratories; the foyer and great stair at the Exeter library; the floors, wall inserts, stairs, benches, and details at the Kimbell Art Museum; the lobby and details of the Yale Center for British Art. Even when polished and filled, the depressions inherent in the material make it look worn. When not filled, as Kahn preferred, the depressions collect dirt and grime. Travertine is not precious or pristine or beautiful. It was thus the perfect stone for Kahn, and although it was never specified, Kahn would probably have used travertine in Jerusalem, a city once ruled by Rome.

Kahn's office built a detailed model of the second Hurva, plans were coordinated, and a section was drawn in pen and ink, unlike the other two proposals. Kahn avoided the difficult problem of how to glaze the space, and it is anyone's guess how this would have been solved had the project been built. The light in the space would have been altered by the properties of the glazing materials used, and no doubt by major revisions to the design as it was refined and problems were resolved. The second design seems to be less successful than the others. It was a solution Kahn explored, as he said, "not knowing in what direction it should go."[6]

214 (opposite). Hurva Synagogue, second proposal. View from between pylons into entrance to sanctuary at balcony level.

215 (above). Hurva Synagogue, second proposal. View from pylon on lower level into sanctuary.

216 (opposite). Hurva Synagogue, second proposal. View from pylon on lower level toward adjacent pylons.

217 (above). Hurva Synagogue, second proposal. View from pylon on lower level toward stair structure.

218 (opposite). Hurva Synagogue, second proposal. View from sanctuary on lower level toward balcony and stair.

219 (above). Hurva Synagogue, second proposal. View toward stair at zone between inner and outer structures on lower level.

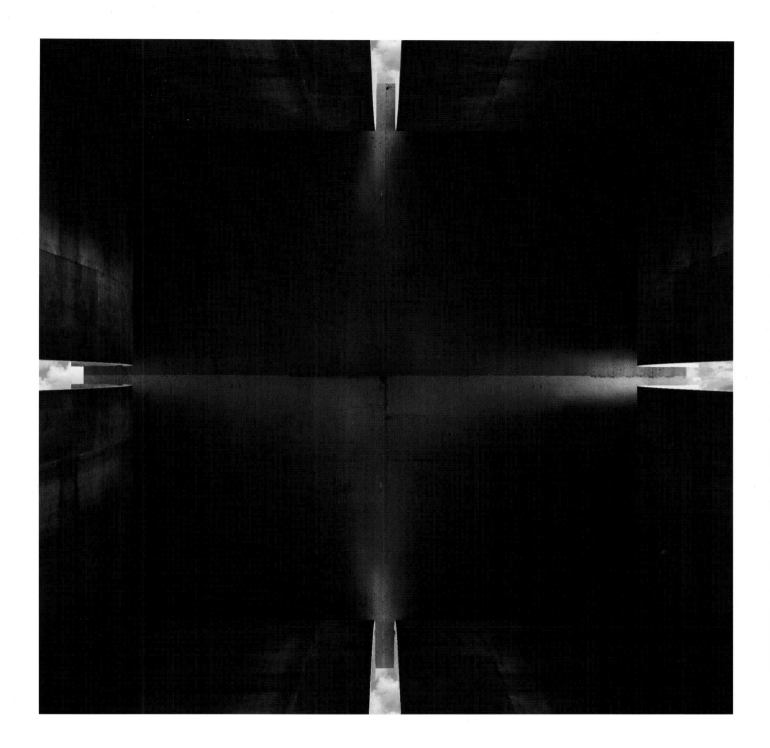

220 (opposite). Hurva Synagogue,
second proposal. View from stair on
lower level.

221 (above). Hurva Synagogue,
second proposal. View up from center
of sanctuary toward curved shell and
ceiling.

Hurva Synagogue, Third Proposal

Jerusalem, Israel, 1973–74

222 (preceding page). Hurva Synagogue, third proposal. View of zone between inner and outer structures.

223 (above). Hurva Synagogue, third proposal. View up from center of sanctuary toward ceiling.

224 (opposite top). Hurva Synagogue, third proposal. Balcony-level plan, 1972.

225 (opposite bottom). Hurva Synagogue, third proposal. First-floor plan, 1972.

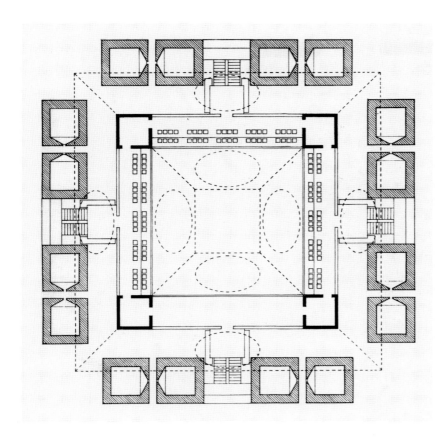

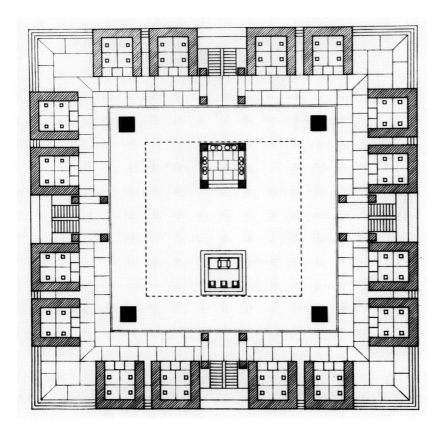

In 1973 Kahn returned to a variation of the initial design for the third and final Hurva Synagogue proposal, while incorporating several elements from the second (figs. 224, 225). The inner sanctuary is supported by four corner columns, as it was in the first, although they are smaller and inset to produce a cantilever, as in the second. Kahn developed a variation of the sloping ceiling planes of the first design and brought light into the sanctuary from above, while eliminating the second-floor ambulatory as he had in the second. In the final proposal, he reintroduced a fixed ark, bema, and seating—although the ark is not the massive wall with niches.

The most striking element of the third proposal is the series of four horizontal cylindrical openings piercing the ceiling planes, shown in a pencil sketch in Kahn's hand (fig. 231). A precedent for the cylindrical openings can be found in an unbuilt version of the central hall of the Phillips Exeter Academy library, developed in 1967 (fig. 229). While the first proposal had independent ceiling sections separated by two-foot-wide slots, this design features a continuous enclosing structure. The square opening created at the center is similar to the ceiling forms of the entry hall at the Yale Center for British Art, developed just prior to the final design of Hurva. The opening is a kind of oculus to the sky, as in the Pantheon.

The final design for Hurva brings together, in a very sophisticated way, the two techniques for controlling light perfected by Kahn: the use of unglazed "ruin" forms to trap light in an intermediate space between interior and exterior to control glare, and the introduction of complex ambient light into the space from openings above.

Memorial Garden
Toward the very end of the Hurva design process—the last few months of Kahn's life—attention was shifted to the development of a memorial garden adjacent to the new Hurva and built around the ruins of the old (fig. 228). It was Jerusalem mayor Teddy Kollek's hope that a successful completion

226 (opposite). Hurva Synagogue, third proposal. View from entrance to sanctuary at balcony level.

227 (below). Hurva Synagogue, third proposal. View from balcony level.

of the garden would permit Hurva to be approved. The correspondence of 1974 is filled with renewed optimism that the project, begun in 1967, might finally get underway in earnest. Kahn wrote to Kollek:

I find that I must visit Jerusalem to spend time on the site of the Hurva, be in your company, and think about the whole thing in the presence of everything around it . . . I tried to design the garden. A garden is a very special thing . . . Please expect me in Jerusalem, within two months or so.[1]

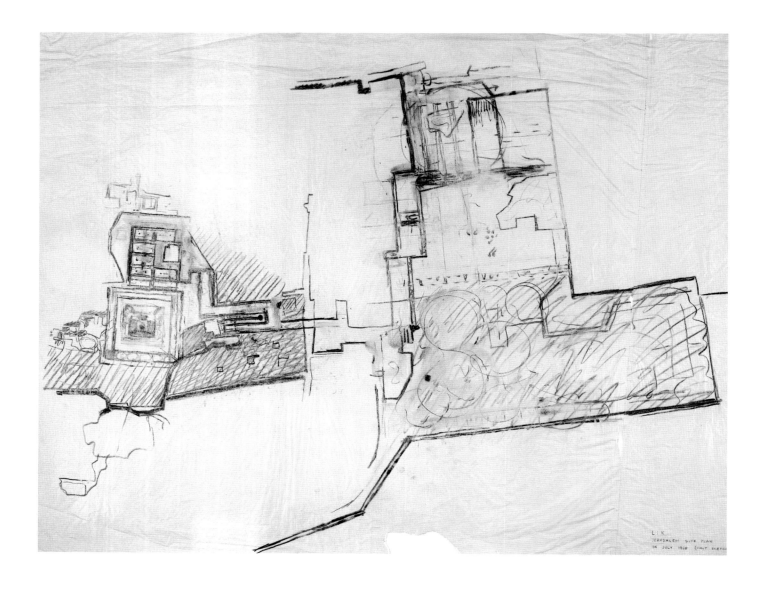

228 (above). Hurva Synagogue, third proposal.
Site plan sketch showing synagogue at left.
Dated 14 July 1968.

229 (right). Library, Phillips Exeter Academy, Exeter,
New Hampshire, 1965–72. Section, unbuilt second
proposal, July 1967.

230 (opposite top). Hurva Synagogue, third
proposal. View from pylon at lower level.

231 (opposite bottom left). Hurva Synagogue,
third proposal. Section sketch. Inscribed Lou K '72.

232 (opposite bottom right). Hurva Synagogue,
third proposal. Section-perspective.

233 (overleaf). Hurva Synagogue, third proposal.
View of sanctuary.

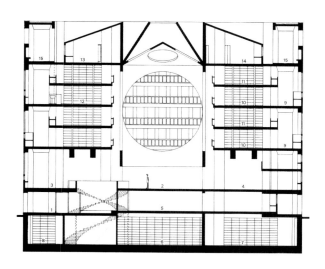

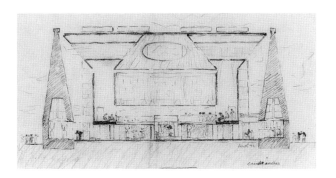

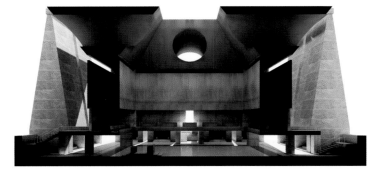

He also wrote:

I visualize the Hurva as a new building, mainly because I am an artist and not an archaeologist. Certainly I don't want to build the new Hurva over the old one, but I picture the walls of the old synagogue being used to enclose a garden area for the new building, adjoining it but remaining a separate entity.[2]

A meeting was finally scheduled for mid-March in New York to develop a strategy for Hurva. Teddy Kollek, who continued as mayor of Jerusalem into the 1990s, wrote Kahn on March 1, 1974, of his desire to begin work on Hurva while he was still in office:

I am eager to start the Hurva during my term of office which will surely be my last. Time is really very pressing and thus I think it is particularly important that we begin the memorial garden now. I warn you that you will be pestered at least once a week on this. I am perfectly convinced that the moment the memorial garden is finished, we can make a decision on Hurva. I hope to see you [next week in New York] and we can discuss all outstanding matters in detail.[3]

Two weeks later, on his way back from an exhausting trip to lecture and inspect the progress of work in Ahmedabad, India, Kahn died in the rest room of New York's Pennsylvania Station. Teddy Kollek wrote to David Wisdom in Kahn's office:

The shock has not subsided. I know how difficult a time this must be for you all. My first thought is to organize a small exhibit in Jerusalem in Louis's memory.[4]

And to Kahn's wife, Esther, Kollek wrote:

Louis's work is a memorial to a great man . . . to our deep regret, the plans have not advanced far enough so that we can execute them. A day before Louis left for Pakistan, I discussed with him at length over the phone his next visit to Jerusalem . . . A date was fixed but alas this was not to be.[5]

The debate over Hurva has continued to this day, with the site still in ruin.

234 (opposite). Hurva Synagogue, third proposal. View at balcony level.

235 (above). Hurva Synagogue, third proposal. View at balcony level.

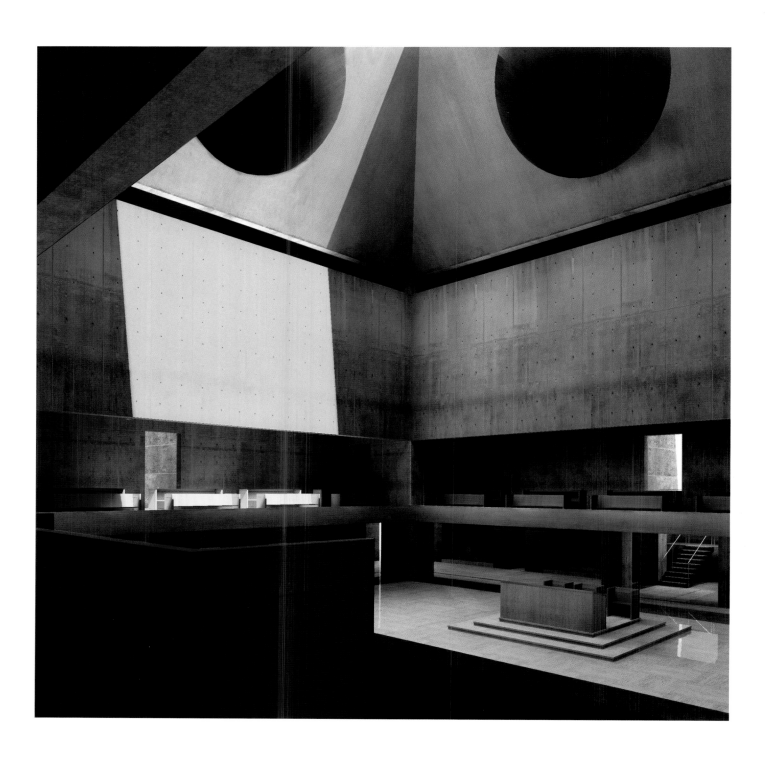

236 (opposite). Hurva Synagogue, third proposal. View of sanctuary from balcony level looking toward ark.

237 (above). Hurva Synagogue, third proposal. View at opening from stair landing to balcony.

238 (above right). Hurva Synagogue, third proposal. View of circular opening through ceiling structure.

239 (overleaf). Hurva Synagogue, third proposal. View from pylon on lower level looking toward sanctuary.

240 (above). Hurva Synagogue, third
proposal. View from stair on lower level
looking toward bema.

241 (opposite). Hurva Synagogue, third
proposal. View from stair on lower level
looking toward adjacent stair.

242 (above). Hurva Synagogue, third proposal. View into pylon niche on lower level.

243 (opposite). Hurva Synagogue, third proposal. Concrete detail.

Palazzo dei Congressi

Venice, Italy, 1968–74

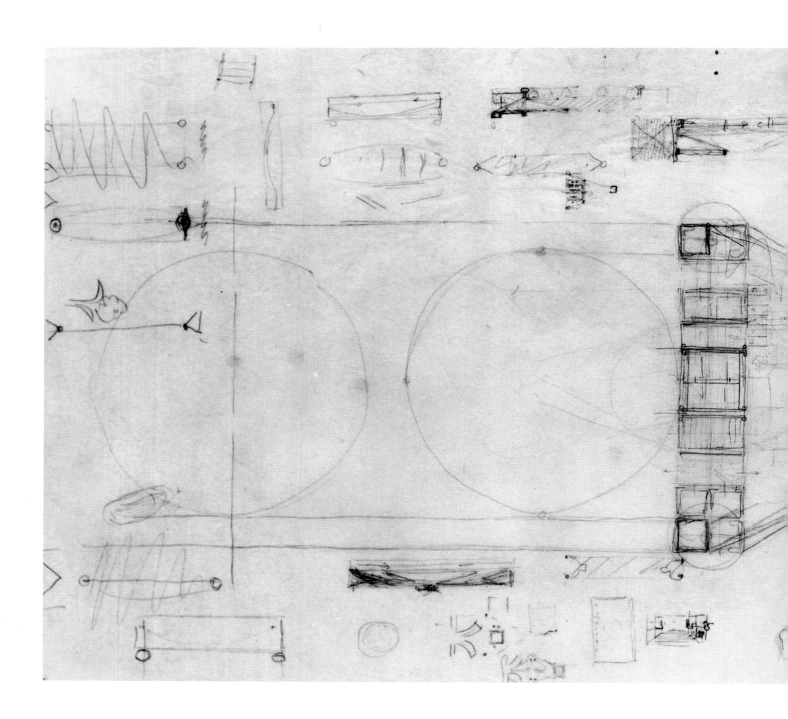

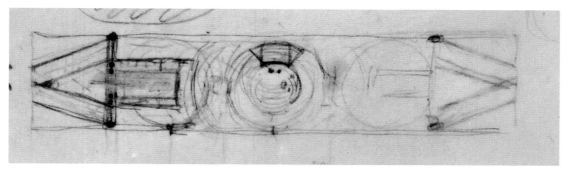

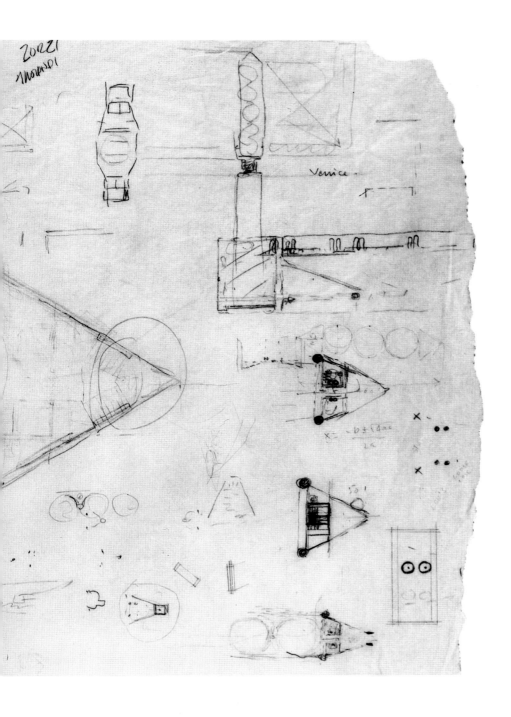

March 1968 was a busy and frustrating time for Kahn. Bids for the Phillips Exeter Academy library had come in far too high, and Kahn was engaged in a struggle to preserve the integrity of the design while reducing costs. The proposal for the Kimbell Art Museum was undergoing major changes, largely to lower construction estimates. The capital complex at Dacca was in construction, and Kahn was under great pressure from Bangladesh to resolve the difficult problem of the roof design of the assembly hall. Construction for the classroom building at Ahmedabad was soon to begin, but Kahn was being criticized in India for inadequate drawings and an incomplete design. Drawings were underway for the Dominican Mother House, but the project would soon see drastic cutbacks in an unsuccessful attempt to salvage it. The Memorial to Six Million Jewish Martyrs was approved by the New York City Art Commission, but the process would quickly collapse due to insufficient funding. In addition, the very first ideas for the unbuilt Hurva Synagogue in Jerusalem were beginning to be studied.

At the same time, Kahn was invited to develop a design for the Palazzo dei Congressi in Venice. A well-known Venetian professor of art history, Giuseppe Mazzariol, had been asked by the Azienda Autonoma di Soggiorno e Turismo, the Venetian tourist agency, to select an architect for the project. In an article for *Lotus*, Mazzariol wrote, "On the name of an architect, I must confess that I didn't have even a moment's uncertainty."[1]

The commission Mazzariol offered to Kahn was to construct a meeting hall that would seat 2,500 to 3,000 people. The new building was to be located at the Giardini Pubblici, or public gardens, long the site of the Venice Biennale, a biannual international art exhibition. The gardens were one of the rare open green areas of Venice, with beautiful allées of trees along the Canale di San Marco designed by G. Antonio Selva in the early eighteenth century.[2] There was no detailed program for the project, and its elements evolved as Kahn developed the design.

244 (preceding page). Palazzo dei Congressi. View of "street" on congress hall level.

245 (opposite top). Palazzo dei Congressi. Plan studies of first proposal.

246 (opposite bottom). Palazzo dei Congressi. Plan study of first proposal.

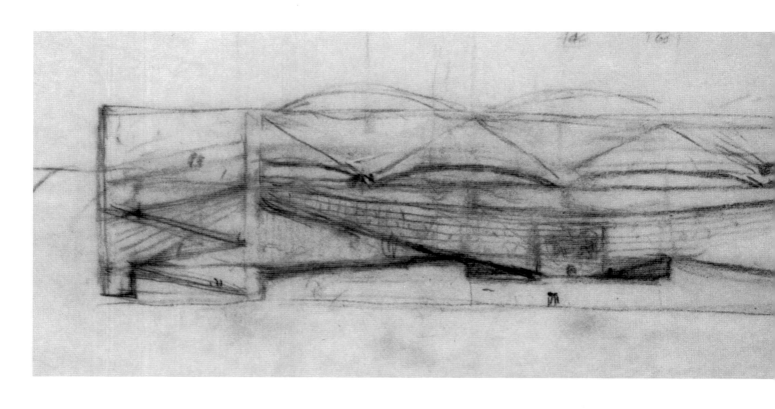

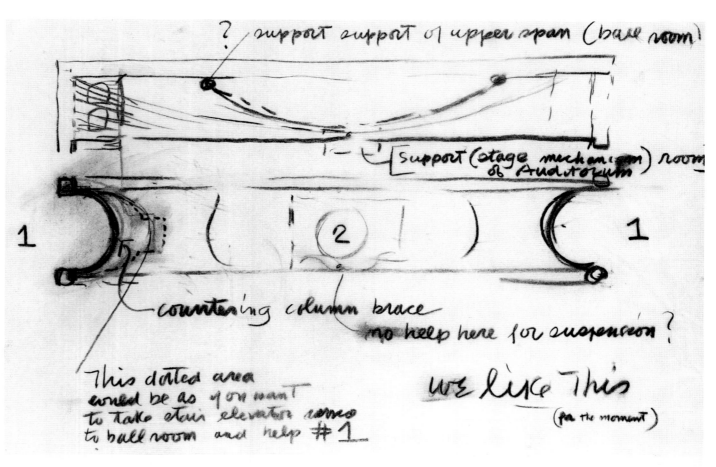

First Proposal

Aware of the difficult soil conditions and repeated flooding of Venice, Kahn made an early decision to support the entire structure in the air, with loads carried on just two caissons set deep to firm foundations. Kahn's earliest sketches of the project show a long slender structure with three domes and triangular supports at each end (figs. 245–47). Many variations of this idea were quickly studied, including curved and rectilinear supports. A diagrammatic sketch indicating tension elements similar to a suspension bridge includes a note that says much about the iterative design process of Kahn's office: "We like this (for the moment)" (fig. 248). The Palazzo dei Congressi, however, was one of the few Kahn projects in which the original design idea remained essentially intact to the end.

By the time of Kahn's first public presentation of the scheme in January 1969, three buildings had found their way into the proposal: the suspended Palazzo dei Congressi, a building to house the Biennale exhibits, and a much smaller gatehouse near the banks of the canal (fig. 251). A large model of the site shows the massing of the buildings, the trees of the gardens, and the domes and arches of the palazzo. The exterior detail and the development of the interior space were largely left for a later time. A single perspective underlay roughing out the major elements of the interior of the meeting hall was begun by a draftsman, but it was never completed (fig. 249).

A major presentation to a large audience was scheduled for Kahn's first public display of the design. A press release prepared by the Azienda indicates the importance attached to the new Palazzo dei Congressi:

On Thursday, the 30th of January, in the Ducal Palace of Venice, Louis Kahn will present to an international audience his plan for the new conference building. This important project is being proposed as part of the plan to give new life to Venice as an international cultural center and as capital of the Veneto Region . . .

247 (opposite top). Palazzo dei Congressi. Section study of first proposal, 1968.

248 (opposite bottom). Palazzo dei Congressi. Study of structural system, plan, and section. Undated.

If Venice is, for its historical traditions and its cultural environment, the ideal place for men to meet each other, Kahn's building fulfills this need for a new policy for Venice in the modern world. This is the first important piece of new town planning, together with that of Le Corbusier for the Venice of the Future, whose historic center must be preserved intact.

Louis Kahn is the only living architect who could have been [called] upon to work for Venice because he is, more than most, away from passing architectural fashions. [He] believes in architecture as a permanent expression of our age. In a city such as Venice, only an architect who still believes in the eternal values of architecture could be invited to replan such an important part of the city . . .

For his project Louis Kahn has asked no fees: It is a gift presented by this great architect to the City of Venice.[3]

Also preserved in a second press release from the Azienda is a complete and concise explanation of the project in Kahn's own words—the text of his presentation to the gathering of approximately five hundred people.[4] Of the Palazzo dei Congressi, Kahn said:

I can see the Congress Hall as if it were a theater in the round—where people look at people—it is not like a movie theater where people look at a performance. My first idea, regardless of the shape of the site, was to make so many concentric circles with a nucleus in the middle. Because the site is long and narrow, I simply sliced the theater in the round with two parallel cuts and it would still retain good visibility from everywhere. Therefore the impression in the hall will be of people seeing people. The curve of the meeting hall is slight in order to retain the sense that it is really a street-like-piazza gently sloping. One could be reminded of the Palio Square in Sienna, which was also created to give it the character of a civic theater.

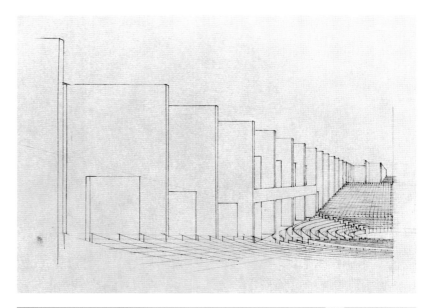

249 (top). Palazzo dei Congressi. Interior perspective study of congress hall. Undated.

250 (above). Palazzo dei Congressi. View of "street" on congress hall level.

251 (opposite). Palazzo dei Congressi. Site plan showing the Biennale exhibit building, the Palazzo dei Congressi, and the gate house. Winter 1968.

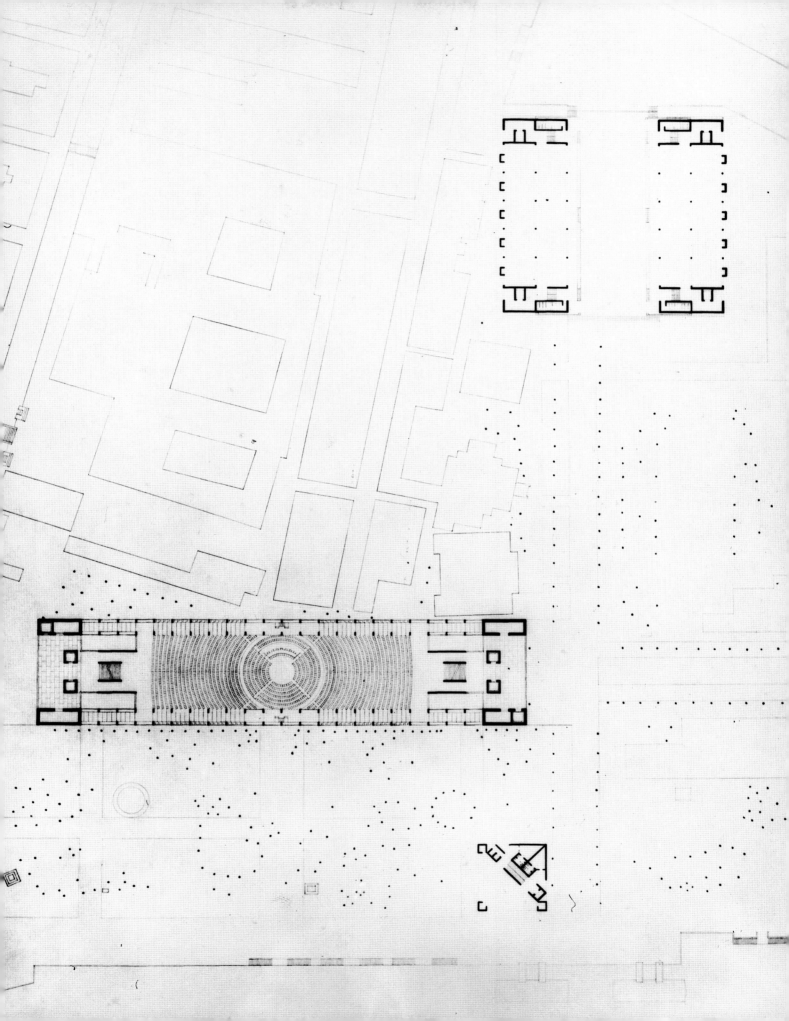

Of the circulation areas serving the hall:

To each side of the hall there are two streets (15 feet wide) which lead to the seating place. These two streets are actually in the inside of beams which carry the structure. These two side streets communicate throughout the entire length of the auditorium and are also connected to the reception hall on the second floor. The hall will hold 2,500 people, but it can be divided in two separate sections for a seating capacity of 1,500 people. Finally the central section could be separated from the rest of the auditorium as a theater in the round for 500 people. The side streets, which lead to the seats, are provided with niches where people can go away from the congress and discuss things separately.

Of the second level (fig. 255):

The reception hall on the second floor is also like a long plaza which is crowned with three domes. The domes are made up of rings of stainless metal and of solid glass, the exterior being covered with lead just as those of St. Mark. The domes also imply that the hall could be divided into three rooms, their size being related to the diameter of the dome above (70 feet). To the sides of this hall, there are series of rooms which again are part of the supporting beams.

Of the rooftop terrace (fig. 254):

The third floor is the roof where the sky is the ceiling. Here you are in the presence of three domes which again tend to divide this terrace into three parts. The parapet which encloses the roof is open to the view of Venice and the lagoon through the crescent openings. On the terrace you will again have on the sides, covered niches where one can shelter.

Of the space below the suspended structure (figs. 256, 257):

The ground floor is a piazza covered by the underside of the auditorium where you can sense the sweep of the structure.

252 (opposite). Palazzo dei Congressi.
View of upper level of congress hall.

253 (above). Palazzo dei Congressi.
View of "street" on congress hall level.

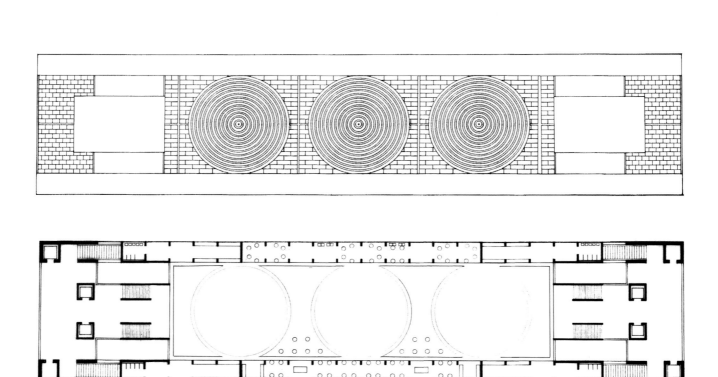

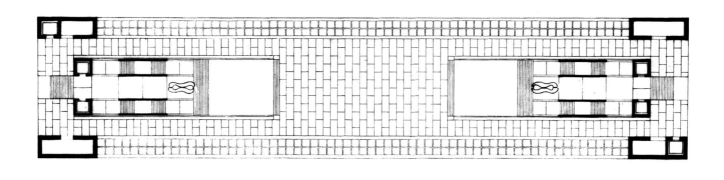

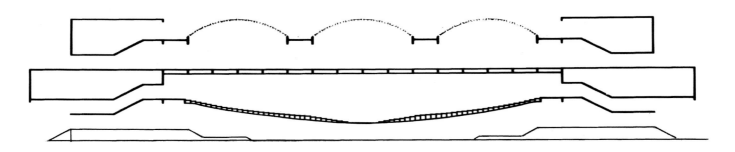

And of the structural system:

The whole structure, reinforced concrete with marble details is conceived like a hanging bridge supported on the two ends by . . . columns, where also the stairs and elevators reach the various levels . . . The Conference Hall is 460 feet long, 78 feet high, and 100 feet wide.

A second structure, the Biennale building, was meant to be used year-round as artist studios and during the Biennale as exhibition space. It was never developed beyond a preliminary schematic idea; a first-floor plan drawn on the site plan and a few sketches in perspective are all that exist in the Kahn Collection to describe this proposal (fig. 260). In his presentation, Kahn said:

The Biennale Building is made of two sections facing each other, divided by a square. Both ends of the square are open: one [to] the widening of the canal, offering a broad water entrance to the Biennale, and the other to the gardens. This allows the gardens to enter the piazza. Each section is two hundred feet long, sixty feet wide, and sixty feet high. Each side contains, on the ground floor, workshop-studios and shops; they will also serve to fit up the court for whatever may be created there on the theme of a happening. On the first floor there are galleries for exhibitions and on the second there are studios for artists.

These buildings should actively be used throughout the year as a free self-supervised academy, as a free community of involvement and exchange. [It will reflect] the spirit of the Biennale depending on the experience, discussion and work done in them. These buildings would still be used by the Biennale for exhibition purposes when it takes place every two years.

The square, 80 feet wide, can be closed at each end by two moving doors 50 feet high and 40 feet wide. A movable roof framed in glass and metal can enclose the square.

Kahn then presented his ideas for the gardens and for an entrance building:

The Entrance Building by the lagoon (50 x 50 x 50 feet high) is a signature building which will personify the meaning of the Congress Hall. It will act as an information center, and [be] used for other services such as restaurant, etc.

The gardens should be a site for rest among the trees and should make available more grass areas (without fences) and places to sit. It should be a park more than a formal garden.

Finally, Kahn presented his thoughts on working in Venice. Le Corbusier had died two years earlier, and his unbuilt proposal for the Venice Hospital was still current:

Venice is an architecture of joy. I like the place as a whole where each building contributes to the other. An architect building in Venice must think in terms of sympathy; working [on] my project I was constantly thinking as if I were asking each building I love so much in Venice whether they would accept me as their company. It was an honor for me to be asked to work in Venice, also because Le Corbusier has produced such an important design for the city. Although I have never been taught personally by Le Corbusier, I have always considered him my teacher—not one to copy, but one in whom the spirit of architecture has not lost his continuity from the past. The great masters of the past are my most honored teachers: Brunelleschi, Bramante, Michelangelo, Palladio.

Kahn's drawings and models were exhibited at the Ducal Palace following the presentation. According to a letter to Kahn from Mazzariol, the exhibition was well attended and covered positively by the local press. A long article in Paris's *Le Monde*, several days after Kahn's presentation, began:

"Venice is not a dying city, but a city which wants to live" . . . Such tragic speech is often used in meetings where the future of this city is to be discussed. And there was no exception for the ceremony programmed for the presentation by the American Architect Louis Kahn of his model of the project for a new Congress Hall for Venice . . . as a last attempt to "rescue" the city.[5]

254 (opposite top). Palazzo dei Congressi, first proposal. Roof-terrace-level plan, 1968.

255 (opposite second from top). Palazzo dei Congressi, first proposal. Reception-hall-level plan, 1968.

256 (opposite third from top). Palazzo dei Congressi, first proposal. Ground-level plan, 1968.

257 (opposite bottom). Palazzo dei Congressi, first proposal. Section, 1968.

258 (above). Palazzo dei Congressi. View toward seating area from "street."

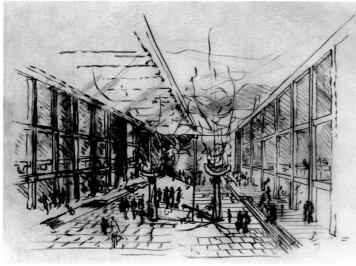

The article went on to discuss the unique attributes of Venice, its problems with flooding and erosion, Le Corbusier's unbuilt proposal for a regional hospital in Venice, and the local political environment. Of Kahn's Palazzo dei Congressi, the writer said:

His Congress Hall . . . should create a center for life and meeting, according to the very character of the town of Venice . . . Louis Kahn considers the entire philosophy of the "human city" within his conception of the Congress Hall. Do not expect, when asking a building from him, to get only a building. He is no builder. He is an Architect in the deepest sense . . . To Louis Kahn, Architecture is Art, and Art is God's language.

But, breaking away from the classical and decorative equilibrium of the Venetian Architecture, Louis Kahn proposes a quiet and monumental Architecture . . . In an era where problems of quantity have first to be solved, such Architecture is rare and lonely. Venice, by building . . . Louis Kahn's Congress Hall would undoubtedly . . . be offered . . . a new chance to survive.

Revisions to the First Proposal

In September of that same year, the Venetian Council heard a request from the Azienda to build Kahn's proposal for the Palazzo dei Congressi in the public gardens, but the process was manipulated by opponents to prevent the application from coming to a vote. Despite this setback and despite a large unpaid invoice, Kahn continued to work on the project. He had structural engineer August Komendant evaluate the structure, and engineering studies of the suspension system for the palazzo were developed. Kahn revised the facades to accommodate his engineer's suggestions. The year following Kahn's death, Komendant provided some insight into Kahn's design process in the book *18 Years with Architect Louis I. Kahn:*

Kahn . . . had promised to do something that would be economically feasible. He showed me three or four sketches on tracing paper. He explained to me what he meant and asked me to study the structural possibilities and economy of the ideas. Kahn was right, to obtain economy, the foundations had to be the minimum. That meant only two open caissons sunk to bedrock about 180 feet below grade. The overbridging of the long distance between the caissons was feasible only by a combination of a suspension system and box-type two-hinged post-tensioned frame, one at each side.

After his return [from presenting the project in Venice], he showed me the design which had been accepted enthusiastically. I did not like the railing because it dominated too strongly the suspension chord. Also, the openings in the box-girder frame were structurally wrong and I said so to Kahn. Furthermore, the shape of the suspension chord looked like a spring which, of course, is not the case. It must be as indicated on my drawing. Kahn was surprised and asked, "Is not a suspension chord of this type also acting as a spring? And say, why are these three large arched openings wrong?" I explained that the openings are located on the compression line of the frame and will crash due to the relatively high shear and compressive stresses . . . He agreed.[6]

259 (opposite top). Palazzo dei Congressi. View of congress-hall-level seating area.

260 (opposite bottom). Palazzo dei Congressi. Interior perspective of Biennale exhibit building, 1968

261 (above). Palazzo dei Congressi. Detail at "street" on congress hall level.

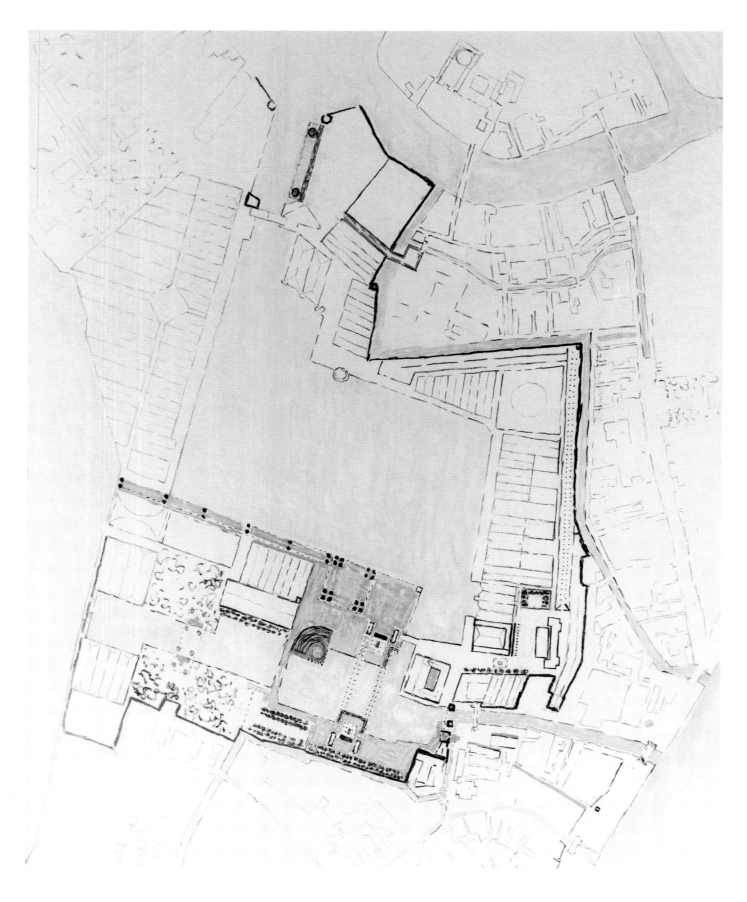

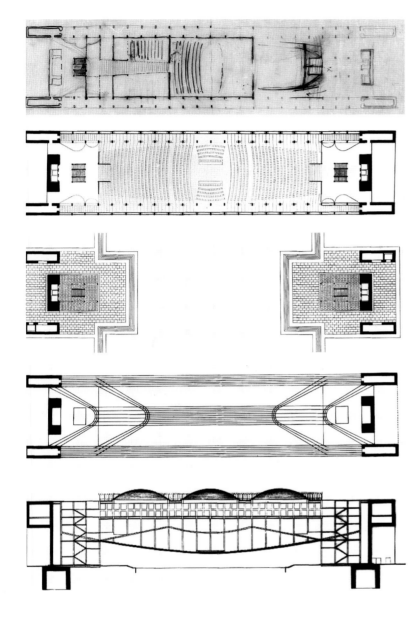

262 (opposite). Palazzo dei Congressi, second proposal. Site plan spanning Canale delle Galeazze, 1974.

263 (top). Palazzo dei Congressi, second proposal. Sketch of mezzanine-level plan, 1974.

264 (second from top). Palazzo dei Congressi, second proposal. Congress-hall-level plan, 1974.

265 (third from top). Palazzo dei Congressi, second proposal. Canal-level plan, 1974.

266 (fourth from top). Palazzo dei Congressi, second proposal. Diagram of cable suspension system, 1974.

267 (above). Palazzo dei Congressi, second proposal. Section, 1974.

Arsenale Proposal

Kahn did no more work on the project for the next year and a half. In 1972 he was invited to participate in a special Biennale exhibition devoted to the city of Venice. It is unclear what, if any, correspondence took place between Kahn and the Azienda in the intervening time, but the proposed site of the palazzo had been moved to a depressed industrial area called the Venice Arsenale. This new location had a number of clear advantages over the Giardini Pubblici site: there was no controversy regarding possible harm to the precious trees of the gardens, the site was available, and the palazzo could become a true bridge structure spanning an expanse of water—the Canale delle Galeazze (fig. 262).

Kahn seized on the possibilities of this new site. The Palazzo dei Congressi was now an academic exercise, and he worked on a revised scheme all but independent of the Azienda. The new design was developed in somewhat greater detail. The theater-in-the-round seating that Kahn had so emphasized in his original presentation was replaced with a more workable curved arrangement (fig. 264). Each caisson base projects into the canal with continuous steps up from the water, in a manner very sympathetic to the gondola culture of the city (fig. 265). Komendant's office prepared a study of the suspension structure necessary to carry the loads of the hall above (fig. 266).

The major revision to the original proposal, however, was the addition of an entirely new level between the large meeting hall on the first level and the reception hall under the three domes at the third level. This intermediate floor contains three smaller meeting/ lecture rooms with raked seating (fig. 263). The underside of this floor creates a curved ceiling in the center of the meeting hall and a sloping ceiling at each end (fig. 267). Kahn's new presentation was displayed at a Biennale exhibit called "Four Projects for Venice" along with other proposals for the city by Frank Lloyd Wright, Le Corbusier, and Isamu Noguchi. Any prospect for the construction of the Palazzo dei Congressi had actually ended several years before.

Financial Concerns

The contemporary observer of Kahn's unbuilt projects, far removed from the day-to-day routine of his architectural practice, naturally tends to focus on missed opportunities. It is easy to overlook the fact that each project that came to an uncomfortable end did so accompanied by frustrating budget problems, unsympathetic committees, petty bureaucrats, political barriers, or unpaid bills.

Two concurrent themes arise from the boxes of correspondence for the Palazzo dei Congressi: the idealism of grand architectural ambitions, and the mundane frustrations of architect-client relations. Often, both are expressed simultaneously. Kahn had no better success at collecting fees than the average practitioner. By his own admission, he was not skilled in the running of a business, and his office rarely had sufficient financial resources. Generously, but perhaps unwisely, Kahn had waived his normal architectural fee for the Palazzo dei Congressi and requested that only direct expenses be paid. He received a check for $20,000 prior to the presentation, but soon afterward he submitted an invoice for an additional $44,000—a low fee even by the standards of 1969. A month and a half after the presentation at the Ducal Palace, Kahn wrote to the president of the Azienda Autonoma di Soggiorno e Turismo, Vito Chiarelli, expressing his obvious frustration:

The work to complete the initial project for the Palazzo dei Congressi as exhibited took many hours and many hands. Architects, in general, have no reserves to finance such projects. If it is possible to arrange that payment be made now of one half of the total balance, this would be very agreeable. The remaining sum we leave to your best arrangement as to payment, possibly within three months.[7]

Chiarelli had introduced Kahn at the Ducal Palace presentation with elaborate praise both of Kahn's stature in the architectural community and of the suitability of his design for Venice. The rather cold and bureaucratic language of Chiarelli's reply to

268. Palazzo dei Congressi. View of congress hall level from "street."

269 (left). Palazzo dei Congressi. View of congress hall level from "street."

270 (overleaf). Palazzo dei Congressi. View of congress hall.

Kahn's letter, however, must have seemed alien to the architect:

We have received your requests in reference to payment and we cannot (over)emphasize the actual detailed conditions in which the Azienda finds itself. We are in the process of perfecting a series of contracts with other institutions of the city with the purpose of putting in motion in concrete terms the passage to the executive phase of the project, and once this operation is perfected, even the financial part will come as a result. We are aware, dear Maestro, of your requests, even if we cannot conceal to you that the Council of Administration has expressed some perplexity about the costs which have become higher than those which in case of similar presentations are common in the city.[8]

By May 16, Kahn still had not received the second payment. He wrote a letter to his greatest advocate in Venice, Giuseppe Mazzariol, briefly touching on the issue of payment but quickly turning to architectural matters:

I have written to President Chiarelli in answer to a letter he sent us requesting that we wait for the payment of the full cost of our presentation. Apparently difficulties have arisen . . . [He] places his hopes in clearing the way for payment by establishing the formal architect-client relationship . . . It would be most marvelous to enter this phase of study for the delight in the unraveling of all the potentialities of expression. I have been thinking along richer lines.[9]

Mazzariol replied several days later, obviously angry at the treatment his friend was receiving:

I personally am of the opinion that you [should] send to President Chiarelli . . . an official letter of admonition . . . I can not hide my bitterness and surprise at the Agency's failure to liquidate, at the moment of the presentation of the project, the sums which you, with great generosity, had decided to limit to the pure and simple expenses incurred by you for the making of the project and models . . . I hope that you, man of great humanness, did understand that besides the profound admiration for your work as an architect, I am

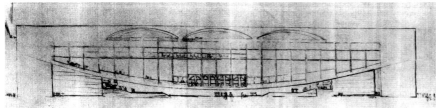

*bound to you also by the reality of great and sin-
cere affection.*[10]

Another letter from Chiarelli did not go very
far in answering the concerns of both Kahn
and Mazzariol. Six months after Kahn's
presentation, Chiarelli in effect blamed the
payment delay on Kahn's inadequate
accounting and the lack of technical information for a proposal that was only
schematic:

*I cannot conceal that I have found myself incon-
venienced because of the lack of a precise plan of
cost for the realization of the project itself,
[which is] difficult to draw out from the material in our hands. In this regard, I would appreciate if you could work out and estimate, if even
schematic, of the cost for the architectural part
only, and also useful data [material and construction techniques] . . .*

*As for the proposal made of your letter of May 16
. . . it would be advisable to separate the material cost of the exhibit (professional services, craft
services, materials and misc. services, shipping
cost, traveling expenses) from the project direct
personnel cost. In that sense, I would appreciate
two (2) separate invoices.*[1]

The correspondence file in the Kahn
Collection is filled with at least seventeen
letters and telegrams dealing with the
$44,000 outstanding balance. The bill was
never paid.[12]

Toward a New Direction
The Palazzo dei Congressi is perhaps most
important for prefiguring an entirely new
direction in Kahn's work. Only the most
schematic of elevations were developed, but
studies clearly indicate that Kahn was thinking of a radical departure for the palazzo.
Here he abandoned the ruin-like outer
building he had used in nearly all his work
since the U.S. Consulate at Luanda. The
brick, concrete, or stone enclosure, where
glass is either hidden or absent, is gone.
Facade studies and a model of the palazzo
are particularly telling (figs. 272–74). They
hint at a system of flush glass, stainless-steel
mullions, and flat metal panels very much

like that used in the Yale Center for British Art—a commission Kahn received almost one year after the palazzo model was built (fig. 275). Of the Yale Center, completed after Kahn's death in 1974, Vincent Scully wrote:

Most of all, however, the magic is in the glass, which Kahn had avoided and tried to subordinate all his life. Now the glass comes alive as an incandescent, reflective material. On the exterior, he presents it cleanly and without detailing, and the stainless steel panels are so matte in finish that the glass surface explodes with light . . . reflecting all the buildings across from it . . . One wonders whether Kahn would have gone further in that essential direction if he had survived.[13]

But for a twist of fate, these words could have been written of the Palazzo dei Congressi, with the city of Venice reflected in its facade.

274 (top). Palazzo dei Congressi, first proposal. Exterior perspective study, 1968.

275 (left). Yale Center for British Art, Yale University, New Haven, Connecticut, 1969–74. Detail of exterior curtain wall.

276 (opposite). Palazzo dei Congressi. View of "street" on congress hall level.

Afterword: Contenders

William J. Mitchell

"I could have been a contender," breathes Marlon Brando in the scene that everyone remembers from *On the Waterfront*. If things had gone differently at a crucial point in the past, then things would be very different now. The line evokes a poignant image of what might have been.

The beautiful computer-generated plates in this volume are more explicit. They actually show us, in photorealistic detail, what we would have had if some of the most compelling designs of Louis Kahn had been carried through to construction. They are a joy, but one tempered with regret. Kent Larson's images reveal that these projects could have played a much more significant cultural role than they turned out to have had. If they had been constructed, they could have been contenders.

Pictures of Possibilities

A fingerprint is an image of a real thing—a fingertip. Its referent is obvious. But what does it mean to make apparently realistic images of things that do not physically exist, as Larson has done here? What can such images be showing us? How do we know whether we can rely on the evidence that they present? What are the rules of this curious game?

To begin to answer these questions, we must make some careful distinctions among the many different uses of images. The practice of photojournalism, for example, depends upon the presumption that photographs function as factual assertions—that they correctly specify the way things were, at some particular spot, at some precise moment in the past. Thus a newspaper photograph might tell us: the suit that President Clinton wore in Washington yesterday *was* blue. But a Webcam image on my computer screen works a little differently; it might, for instance, establish: the sky *is* blue in Sydney right now. An architectural perspectivist's rendering might assert: this building's curtain wall *will be* blue. A book illustration might present a fiction: a unicorn's eyes *are* blue. A digitally manipulated photograph in a fashion magazine might propagate a falsehood: a model's eyes *are* blue. And the photorealistic images in this book should be understood as claims: if these Kahn buildings had been constructed, then they *would have* looked like this.

Philosophers classify these "if . . . then" constructions as counterfactual conditionals. The premise is not true, but it might have been; the buildings were not actually constructed, but it is not hard to imagine that things could have proceeded otherwise. The conclusion then describes something that would logically have followed—an unrealized possibility. Of course, there is no limit to the number of counterfactual premises we might state, and the consequences we might then derive from them. The exercise becomes interesting only when the "might have" is highly plausible, when the conclusion follows rigorously from it according to sound principles of logic, and when this conclusion is not a triviality—when it illuminates our history or our current condition in some worthwhile way. Kent Larson's images are not only beautiful, they also meet these tests.

First, the premises satisfy the requirement of plausibility. In all cases, these buildings were designed with the intention of actual construction. Circumstances intervened to thwart those intentions. But it certainly is not gratuitous to imagine the enterprises of Kahn and his clients succeeding rather than failing.

Second, the derivation of consequences is appropriately meticulous and rigorous, and it is here that Larson has made his most original contribution. He has gone to the primary documents—Kahn's drawings and other relevant evidence—carefully constructed three-dimensional CAD models from them, specified appropriate material properties and lighting conditions, and finally employed advanced visualization software to construct detailed, accurate, photorealistic perspective images from specified viewpoints. This is a process that demands both careful scholarship and shrewd application of the most advanced computer-graphics technology.

Last, we can be grateful for the way in which these images advance the discourse of architecture. They allow us, at last, to appreciate fully some of Louis Kahn's most profound explorations of the interactions of geometry, materiality, and light. Of course, we could always examine the drawings and models that Kahn left. But this is different; it is like hearing an orchestra perform some well-known but never-played score for the first time. Everyone who cares about architecture can learn from the results of Larson's labors.

Creating the Digital Models

It would be convenient if the documents describing unbuilt architectural designs were complete and consistent, but they never are. So the first step in creating computer reconstructions is to fill in missing information and resolve ambiguities and inconsistencies in whatever documents can be found. This is a demanding scholarly task—one closely akin to that faced by an editor trying to produce a definitive text of a literary work such as *Ulysses*. And it risks similar potential for controversy.

One source of this problem is the way in which architectural designs evolve over time from quick, rough sketches through design development and eventually to relatively complete and detailed construction documents. But even fully developed construction documents make implicit assumptions about prevailing construction practices in particular contexts and have to be interpreted in the light of extensive knowledge of these practices. Furthermore, many important details may never be described completely in the documents; they are left, instead, to be resolved on site during the actual construction process. Thus, when a design is abandoned at any point short of the actual building's completion, the result is a body of information that leaves many blanks to be filled in.

A second difficulty is that designers, at any stage in a project, are engaged in a process of developing, exploring, and eventually choosing among alternatives. When a project is abandoned, it is not always clear which (if any) of the alternatives represented in the documentation should be taken as definitive. This may create ambiguities at many levels—from that of overall layout to that of construction details and material choices.

Perhaps the most subtle dilemmas of all result from the fact that most incomplete designs contain logical inconsistencies. These may be gross—as when windows appear in different positions in plan and elevation, or columns do not align from floor to floor—or they may only come to light after an extensive process of collecting, organizing, and deriving indirect consequences from the available information. Usually it is not that the designer was incompetent or incapable of recognizing such difficulties but that designing a building involves developing many loosely coordinated ideas about geometry, construction, and materials in parallel. Sometimes, as well, the logical consequences of an apparently innocuous design move may not be apparent immediately and may not show up until much later. So much of the intellectual activity in designing revolves around identifying and resolving inconsistencies in concepts as they evolve; if the process is terminated prematurely, it is very likely that many inconsistencies will remain. These may be things that the designer would have resolved quickly and straightforwardly if there had been a chance to get around to them, or they may raise deep and difficult problems. In any case they all must be sorted out.

Before a design is actually executed, these various difficulties must be resolved; the construction information must be complete and consistent (to some reasonable practical degree) if on-site problems, and perhaps lawsuits, are to be avoided. A similarly complete and consistent three-dimensional CAD model must be produced before photorealistic computer renderings or animations of an unbuilt project can be generated. If this rigorous standard is not met, the model may not even render, or if it does, it will certainly not produce a satisfactory result. To generate the images in this book, then, Kent Larson had to study Louis Kahn's intentions and techniques, understand the relevant construction practices, and eventually try to complete and resolve the projects as if he were Kahn himself.

Materials and Light

Once a satisfactory three-dimensional geometric model of a project has been created, the next step is to establish surface properties and lighting conditions with meticulous care. This task may be carried out at varying levels of aspiration.

If only simple shaded images are desired—similar to those of early Renaissance paintings—one can describe each surface by means of a few numbers that specify its color and reflectivity. But if one also wants to convey subtle qualities of materiality as revealed by light—as, for example, in the paintings of Vermeer—each surface's microstructure must be specified in detail. In other words, information must be provided about textures and edge conditions. Larson has done this, on these pages, by employing the technique of texture mapping; he begins with a library of photographed textures, then employs specialized software to map these photographs onto surfaces in the model—a process analogous to that of wallpapering the surfaces of a room.

The starting point is a close study of Louis Kahn's palette of materials and his principles of material use. In some cases, material choices are explicit in the available design documents, and the texture-mapping task is thus relatively straightforward. But in other cases, the choices are implicit, or are left completely undefined, and must then be guessed at in light of context and available evidence.

When the materials have been decided, the texture mapper must bring a craftsperson's eye and much patience to the job of positioning textures on surfaces. Texture patterns must be correctly scaled and aligned. Curvature distortions must be avoided. Joints must be made seamlessly. Implausible repetitions must not be allowed. Edges must be handled correctly. Getting all this exactly right requires a close knowledge of actual materials, fabrication processes, and construction practices—of the generative factors that yield *real* textures. If one wants to specify brick textures correctly, for example, one must know about bonding, mortar joints, and how corners are formed. If one wants to make concrete surfaces look plausible, one must know about formwork, concrete mixes, and reinforcement.

Finally, the spatial and spectral characteristics of the various light sources—both natural and artificial—must be defined. If the ambition is to reveal nuances and intricacies of materiality and light, as was crucial in these studies of Kahn, then this must be done in considerable detail. And it is important to be not only plausible but nitpickingly accurate; if one merely wants to produce images that look convincing, the sun can be positioned anywhere, but if one is showing a building oriented in a specific way on a particular site in Jerusalem, then one must calculate a sun altitude and azimuth that might actually occur.

The Virtual Camera

The computer-graphics software that was used to produce the final images employs the metaphor of the "virtual camera." It permits the specification of viewing parameters in terms of familiar camera settings such as station point, direction of view, and angle of view, and then computes a shaded perspective view accordingly. The result looks very much like a corresponding photograph of the actual scene.

At the stage of specifying viewing parameters, then, it is necessary to think like an architectural photographer and ask the questions that would arise on a shoot. What viewpoints will work best? What lighting conditions will be most revealing? Should wide-angle or telephoto shots be created? It is more like studio work than location photography, however, since conditions can be controlled with great precision. There are some additional freedoms: there is no gravity in the digital world, and the "photographer" can squeeze easily into the tightest of spaces, so that viewpoints that in reality would be quite impossible can be shot.

The freedoms of the virtual camera are seductive, but if they are exploited thoughtlessly, they can yield misleading results. In particular, a photorealistic image of an unbuilt architectural work from a physically impossible viewpoint can leave an unwary viewer with a very inaccurate idea of what the actual, on-foot experience of the building would be like. (On the other hand, an image that clearly stood outside the conventions of photorealism, and was overtly conceptual in its intentions, would be far less likely to have this effect.) To avoid such problems, Kent Larson created two distinct image types: views that might have resulted if a flesh-and-blood architectural photographer had carried a view camera to the realized buildings, and clearly impossible images such as the section-perspective. A viewer always knows what is being observed; the conventions are clear and consistent.

Burning Machine Cycles

Although three-dimensional computer-graphics technology has been available since the 1960s, it is only recently that virtual photographs of the quality shown in this book have become feasible. This is because calculating accurately rendered images of complex scenes makes enormous demands on processors and memory. When computers were feeble and expensive, photorealism was not a practical possibility.

But the ongoing effects of Moore's Law—the computer power available at a constant price doubles every eighteen months or so—have radically changed this situation. Now, machine cycles and computer memory are low-cost commodities, and designers can afford to be increasingly ambitious in their computer-graphics efforts. Successive generations of three-dimensional modeling and rendering software have rapidly emerged to exploit this expansion of possibilities.

Once the basic principles of computing shaded perspective images had been established, in the late 1970s, it quickly became clear that most of the complexities in the task of photorealistic rendering of scenes—and the key to verisimilitude—lay in accounting for the extraordinarily complicated interreflections of light from surface to surface. Computationally intensive techniques known as raytracing and radiosity procedures, and numerous variations on them, were developed to accomplish this. Since they are based closely on relevant physical principles, they can produce images that not only look right but genuinely have the status of scientific simulations.

It all came together. These hardware and software advances finally provided the tools that Kent Larson needed to bring his digital models miraculously to life. It took countless hours of computation, but the results are truly a revelation.

On every page of this book, it is possible to see what might have been.

Acknowledgments

Although I did not know it at the time, this book began in 1992 when John Dixon, the editor of *Progressive Architecture*, accepted my proposal to undertake a study of Louis Kahn's unbuilt Hurva Synagogue. Without John's leap of faith—he had only simple line drawings to hint at the possibilities—this project would not have happened. I am grateful to Carter Manny and the Graham Foundation for Advanced Studies in the Fine Arts for the two research grants that supported this effort, and to Vincent Scully, who pointed me toward the importance of the ruin in Kahn's unbuilt work. The ongoing efforts of Julia Converse and William Whitaker of the Architectural Archives of the University of Pennsylvania, as well as unfettered access to the archival material of the Kahn Collection, were essential to this endeavor. Peter L. Gluck, my partner in practice until 1996, offered insightful comments and patiently tolerated this diversion from the work of our firm. Many architects and historians reviewed the work in progress and offered valuable criticism, including James Stewart Polshek, William Porter, Marshall Meyers, Thomas Vreeland, Kenneth Frampton, Stanford Anderson, Peter Reed, and Ram Karmi. Sue Ann Kahn helped me better understand many aspects of her father's work and life. Akira Fujimoto and Koji Tsuchiya of Integra collaborated on the production of the images first published in *P/A* in September 1993. Takehiko Nagakura was a partner in the exploration of new technologies useful for visualizing the unbuilt, and Daniel Brick constructed much of the model for the meeting house of the Salk Institute. Many companies contributed hardware and software to this project, including Silicon Graphics, Sigma Design, Intel, Adobe, and Eastman Kodak. Lightscape, through Stuart Feldman, provided the radiosity-based software used for all of the computer-graphics images in this book, and Dice-LVT provided transparencies. Finally, I am indebted to William J. Mitchell, dean of the MIT School of Architecture and Planning, for encouraging this project and for creating at MIT an all too rare environment that supports research into computation and architecture.

Notes

Foreword

1. It is interesting, to me at least, that when I was for a short time around 1960 acting as an editor for George Braziller's historical series and was able to prevail upon Frank Brown to write the Roman volume, Brown rejected my suggestion that there should be more in it about Roman wall decoration—decorative carving and so on— saying that such would result in "just another Beaux-Arts book about Roman architecture." He was apparently a modernist too, like Kahn, and like him was entranced by the powerful geometric abstraction of the ruin.

Introduction: Unbuilt Ruins

1. Louis Kahn, letter written from the American Academy in Rome, Kahn Collection, University of Pennsylvania, reprinted in Eugene J. Johnson and Michael J. Lewis, *Drawn from the Source: The Travel Sketches of Louis I. Kahn* (Cambridge, Mass.: MIT Press, 1996), 72–73.

2. Louis Kahn, quoted in *Louis I. Kahn: Writings, Lectures, Interviews*, ed. Alessandra Latour (New York: Rizzoli, 1991), 151.

3. Louis Kahn, quoted in Latour, *Louis I. Kahn: Writings, Lectures, Interviews*, 168.

4. Louis Kahn, quoted in Latour, *Louis I. Kahn: Writings, Lectures, Interviews*, 273.

5. Louis Kahn, quoted in Latour, *Louis I. Kahn: Writings, Lectures, Interviews*, 263–64.

6. Louis Kahn, quoted in Latour, *Louis I. Kahn: Writings, Lectures, Interviews*, 313.

7. Louis Kahn, notebook (K12.22), c. 1955, Kahn Collection.

8. Johnson and Lewis, *Drawn from the Source*, 109.

9. Louis Kahn in a conversation with Alison Smithson, in Johnson and Lewis, *Drawn from the Source*, 108.

10. Louis Kahn, quoted in "How'm I Doing, Corbusier? An Interview with Patricia McLaughlin," in Latour, *Louis I. Kahn: Writings, Lectures, Interviews*, 307.

11. Louis Kahn, "Remarks," *Perspecta: The Yale Architectural Journal* 9–10 (1965), reprinted in Latour, *Louis I. Kahn: Writings, Lectures, Interviews*, 206.

12. Marshall Meyers, telephone conversation with the author, August 1, 1993.

U.S. Consulate, Luanda

1. David B. Brownlee and David G. De Long, *Louis I. Kahn: In the Realm of Architecture* (New York: Rizzoli, 1991), 20–22.

2. Vincent Scully, "Louis I. Kahn and the Ruins of Rome," *Engineering and Science* (Pasadena, Calif., Institute of Technology), winter 1993, 5.

3. Vincent Scully, "Louis I. Kahn and the Ruins of Rome," *MoMA: The Members Quarterly of the Museum of Modern Art* 12 (summer 1992): 3.

4. Louis Kahn, "On Monumentality," in *New Architecture and City Planning: A Symposium*, ed. Paul Zucker (New York: New York Philosophical Library, 1944), 77–88.

5. Louis Kahn, letter written from the American Academy in Rome, Kahn Collection, University of Pennsylvania, reprinted in Eugene J. Johnson and Michael J. Lewis, *Drawn from the Source: The Travel Sketches of Louis I. Kahn* (Cambridge, Mass.: MIT Press, 1996), 72–73.

6. Louis Kahn, interview by Michael Graves, originally published in *A+U: Architecture and Urbanism*, November 1983; reprinted in Johnson and Lewis, *Drawn from the Source*, 73.

7. Louis Kahn, handwritten draft of letter to Walter Gropius, undated, responding to a letter from Gropius to Kahn, March 16, 1953, Box LIK 66, Kahn Collection, as quoted in Brownlee and De Long, *Louis I. Kahn: In the Realm*, 56.

8. Louis Kahn, "Talk at the Conclusion of the Otterlo Congress," in *New Frontiers of Architecture: CIAM '59 in Otterlo*, ed. Oscar Newman (New York: Universal Books, 1961), 213.

9. Louis Kahn, quoted in Henry S. F. Cooper, "Dedication Issue: The New Art Gallery and Design Center," *Yale Daily News*, November 6, 1953.

10. Louis Kahn, quoted in Susan Braudy, "The Architectural Metaphysic of Louis I. Kahn," *New York Times Magazine*, November 15, 1970, 86.

11. Louis Kahn, interview, *Perspecta: The Yale Architectural Journal* 7 (1961): 9–18.

12. Kahn, interview, *Perspecta* 7.

13. Kahn, interview, *Perspecta* 7.

14. Louis Kahn, "Remarks," *Perspecta: The Yale Architectural Journal* 9–10 (1965), in *Louis I. Kahn: Writings, Lectures, Interviews*, ed. Alessandra Latour (New York: Rizzoli, 1991), 204.

15. Brownlee and De Long, *Louis I. Kahn: In the Realm*, 68.

Meeting House of the Salk Institute

1. Louis Kahn, quoted in "On Form and Design," *Journal of Architectural Education* 15, no. 3 (fall 1960): 62.

2. Jonas Salk, interviewed for the film *Louis I. Kahn: Silence and Light* (produced by Michael Blackwood).

3. David B. Brownlee and David G. De Long, *Louis I. Kahn: In the Realm of Architecture* (New York: Rizzoli, 1991), 331.

4. Brownlee and De Long, *Louis I. Kahn: In the Realm*, 330–31.

5. Vincent Scully, *Louis I. Kahn* (New York: George Braziller, 1962), 37.

6. Brownlee and De Long, *Louis I. Kahn: In the Realm*, 433.

7. Louis Kahn, quoted in *Louis I. Kahn: Writings, Lectures, Interviews*, ed. Alessandra Latour (New York: Rizzoli, 1991), 150.

8. Scully, *Louis I. Kahn*, 38.

9. Brownlee and De Long, *Louis I. Kahn: In the Realm*, 336.

Mikveh Israel Synagogue

1. Sue Ann Kahn, telephone conversation with the author, 1996.

2. David B. Brownlee and David G. De Long, *Louis I. Kahn: In the Realm of Architecture* (New York: Rizzoli, 1991), 365.

3. Louis Kahn, quoted in *Louis I. Kahn: Writings, Lectures, Interviews*, ed. Alessandra Latour (New York: Rizzoli, 1991), 202–3.

4. Colin Low, 1992 (http://www.digital-brilliance.com/kab/nok/q1.txt), URL, May 1998.

5. Jeffry Keiffer, "Criticism: A Reading of Louis Kahn's Salk Institute Laboratories," *A+U (Architecture and Urbanism)*, April 1993.

6. Joseph Burton, "Notes from Volume Zero: Louis Kahn and the Language of God," *Perspecta: The Yale Architectural Journal* 20 (1983): 89, 90.

7. Eugene J. Johnson and Michael J. Lewis, *Drawn from the Source: The Travel Sketches of Louis I. Kahn* (Cambridge, Mass.: MIT Press, 1996), 95.

8. Louis Kahn, quoted in Latour, *Louis I. Kahn: Writings, Lectures, Interviews*, 90.

9. Louis Kahn, in foreword to Richard Saul Wurman and Eugene Feldman, *The Notebooks and Drawings of Louis I. Kahn* (Falcon Press, 1962).

10. Louis Kahn, quoted in "Law and Rule" (RIBA), quoted in Anne Tyng, *Beginnings: Louis I. Kahn's Philosophy of Architecture* (New York: John Wiley and Sons, 1984), 19.

11. Louis Kahn, letter to Richard Demarco, August 28, 1973, Box LIK 10, Kahn Collection, University of Pennsylvania.

12. Frank E. Brown, *Roman Architecture* (New York: George Braziller, 1961), 9.

13. Vincent Scully, "Louis I. Kahn and the Ruins of Rome," *MoMA: The Members Quarterly of the Museum of Modern Art* 12 (summer 1992): 9.

14. Brown, *Roman Architecture*, 10.

15. Brown, *Roman Architecture*, 27.

16. Brown, *Roman Architecture*, 25, 33.

17. Louis Kahn, Voice of America lectures, reprinted in Vincent Scully, *Louis I. Kahn* (New York: George Braziller, 1962), 115, 116.

18. Kahn, Voice of America lectures, 116.

Memorial to Six Million Jewish Martyrs

1. For a history of the project, see Susan G. Solomon, "Memorial to the Six Million Martyrs," in David B. Brownlee and David G. De Long, *Louis I. Kahn: In the Realm of Architecture* (New York: Rizzoli, 1991), 399–403.

2. Heinz Ronner and Sharad Jhaveri, *Louis I. Kahn: Complete Works 1935–1974* (Basel and Boston: Birkhauser, 1987), 338.

3. Ronner and Jhaveri, *Louis I. Kahn: Complete Works*, 336, 338.

4. Louis Kahn, quoted in "Memorials: Lest We Forget," *Architectural Forum* 129 (December 1968): 15.

5. Solomon, "Memorial to the Six Million Martyrs," 401.

6. Joseph L. Lichten, letter to Louis I. Kahn, reprinted in Solomon, "Memorial to the Six Million Martyrs," 519.

7. Informal contract between Kahn and six members of the committee, January 20, 1968, reprinted in Solomon, "Memorial to the Six Million Martyrs," 519.

8. Ronner and Jhaveri, *Louis I. Kahn: Complete Works*, 338.

Hurva Synagogue, First Proposal

1. David B. Green, "Rising from the Ruin?," *Jewish Report: The Arts*, December 12, 1996, 40–41. (Much of the history of Hurva comes from this article.)

2. Louis Kahn, letter to Yehuda Tamir, Ministerial Committee for Jerusalem, March 28, 1969, with copies to Teddy Kollek, Yaacov Salomon, and Ram Karmi, Box LIK 39, Kahn Collection, University of Pennsylvania.

3. Louis Kahn, letter to Mrs. Serata, Jewish Theological Seminary, New York, July 2, 1968, Box LIK 39, Kahn Collection.

4. Louis Kahn, "Space-Order in Architecture," lecture, Pratt Institute, November 10, 1959.

5. Heinz Ronner and Sharad Jhaveri, *Louis I. Kahn: Complete Works 1935–1974* (Basel and Boston: Birkhauser, 1987), 362–67.

6. Ronner and Jhaveri, *Louis I. Kahn: Complete Works*, 362–67.

7. Ronner and Jhaveri, *Louis I. Kahn: Complete Works*, 362–67.

8. Ronner and Jhaveri, *Louis I. Kahn: Complete Works*, 362–67.

9. Richard Saul Wurman, *What Will Be Has Always Been* (Access Press and Rizzoli, 1986), 217.

10. Louis Kahn, letter to Yaacov Salomon, August 19, 1968, with copies to Teddy Kollek and Ram Karmi, Box LIK 39, Kahn Collection.

11. Teddy Kollek, letter to Louis Kahn, August 29, 1968, Box LIK 39, Kahn Collection.

Hurva Synagogue, Second Proposal

1. Heinz Ronner and Sharad Jhaveri, *Louis I. Kahn: Complete Works 1935–1974* (Basel and Boston: Birkhauser, 1987), 362–67.

2. Louis Kahn, in *Visionary Architects: Boullée, Ledoux, Lequeu* (Houston: University of St. Thomas, 1968), 5.

3. Michel Foucault, "The Eye of Power," in *Power/Knowledge: Selected Interviews and Other Writings, 1972–1977*, ed. Colin Gordon (New York: Pantheon Books, 1980), 253, 154.

4. Louis Kahn, quoted in *Louis I. Kahn: Writings, Lectures, Interviews*, ed. Alessandra Latour (New York: Rizzoli, 1991), 117.

5. Edmund Burke, *A Philosophical Enquiry into the Origins of Our Ideas of the Sublime and Beautiful*, 1759.

6. Ronner and Jhaveri, *Louis I. Kahn: Complete Works*, 363.

Hurva Synagogue, Third Proposal

1. Louis Kahn, letter to Teddy Kollek, January 7, 1974, Box LIK 39, Kahn Collection, University of Pennsylvania.

2. Louis Kahn, letter to Teddy Kollek, 1974, Box LIK 39, Kahn Collection.

3. Teddy Kollek, letter to Louis Kahn, March 1, 1974, Box LIK 39, Kahn Collection.

4. Teddy Kollek, letter to David Wisdom, March 26, 1974, Box LIK 39, Kahn Collection.

5. Teddy Kollek, letter to Esther Kahn, April 8, 1974, Box LIK 39, Kahn Collection.

Palazzo dei Congressi

1. Giuseppe Mazzariol, "Un progetto per Venezia," *Lotus* 6 (1969): 17.

2. Elise Vider, "Palazzo dei Congressi," in David B. Brownlee and David G. De Long, *Louis I. Kahn: In the Realm of Architecture* (New York: Rizzoli, 1991), 405.

3. Azienda Autonoma di Soggiorno e Turismo, Venice, "Louis Kahn's New Conference Center for Venice" (press release), January 30, 1969, Box LIK 36, Kahn Collection, University of Pennsylvania.

4. Azienda Autonoma di Soggiorno e Turismo, Venice, "Louis Kahn Talks about His Project," (press release), undated, Box LIK 36, Kahn Collection.

5. Jacques Michel, "A Cultural Center for the City of Venice, by Louis Kahn: A Great Architect in a Great City," *Le Monde*, February 2, 1969, 15–17, translated for Louis Kahn's files, Box LIK 36, Kahn Collection.

6. August E. Komendant, *18 Years with Architect Louis I. Kahn* (Englewood, N.J.: Aloray, 1975).

7. Louis Kahn, letter to Vito Chiarelli, March 18, 1969, Box LIK 36, Kahn Collection.

8. Vito Chiarelli, letter to Louis Kahn, undated translation, Box LIK 36, Kahn Collection.

9. Louis Kahn, letter to Giuseppe Mazzariol, May 16, 1969, Box LIK 36, Kahn Collection.

10. Giuseppe Mazzariol, letter to Louis Kahn, undated translation, Box LIK 36, Kahn Collection.

11. Vito Chiarelli, letter to Louis Kahn, undated translation, Box LIK 36, Kahn Collection.

12. Vider, "Palazzo dei Congressi," 406.

13. Vincent Scully, "Louis I. Kahn and the Ruins of Rome," *MoMA: The Members Quarterly of the Museum of Modern Art* 12 (summer 1992): 13.

Illustration Credits

Except as noted below, all illustrations have been created by Kent Larson. Numbers refer to figure numbers.

The Architectural Archive, University of Pennsylvania, Gift of Richard Saul Wurman: 114

Izzika Gaon: 153

Louis I. Kahn Collection, University of Pennsylvania and Pennsylvania Historical and Museum Commission: 5, 6, 11, 18, 22, 24, 27–29, 32, 33, 35, 37, 39, 40, 43, 46–48, 52, 60, 72, 77, 84–89, 91, 93, 98–100, 104, 105, 107, 108, 110, 113, 119, 131–37, 140, 144, 146, 149, 151, 152, 159, 162–64, 166, 174, 180, 199, 200, 203, 204, 206, 207, 224, 225, 228, 229, 231, 249, 251, 254–57, 260, 262–67, 273, 274

Louis I. Kahn Collection, University of Pennsylvania and Pennsylvania Historical and Museum Commission (drawing detail): 61, 64–66, 71, 73, 95–97, 197, 245–48

Louis I. Kahn Collection, University of Pennsylvania and Pennsylvania Historical and Museum Commission (photograph by George Pohl): 167

Collection of Sue Ann Kahn: 7–10, 16, 17, 170–72

Kent Larson: 1, 2, 21, 23, 25, 54, 70, 92, 145, 272, 275

The Museum of Modern Art, New York: 115

Collection of Robert Venturi: 109